Religion And Relationship

Minister Dante Fortson

Religion And Relationship

Copyright © 2009 by Minister Dante Fortson
Web Site: www.MinisterFortson.com

ISBN 10: 1-448-69130-3
ISBN 13: 978-1448-69130-2

All scripture quotations in this book are taken from the King James Version of the Bible.

All rights reserved. No portion of this book may be reproduced or transmitted in any form or by any means, electronic or mechanical, including photocopying, recording, or by an information storage and retrieval system, without the written permission of the author.

First Edition. Printed in the United States of America

Editors: Perryetta Lacy, Brian Lacy, Jenelle Jackson, Taneka Dickson
Cover Design: Yessur Media
Website: www.YessurMedia.com

Published By: Image Agenda Media

TABLE OF
Contents

- Acknowledgments
- How To Use This Book   i
- Foreword – Pastor Perryetta Lacy   iii
- Introduction   v
- Pre-Read Assessment Test   ix

- **Chapter One**   1
  - Lucifer's Relationship With Mankind
  - Adam's Punishment
  - Lucifer's Relationship With God
  - What Adam And Satan Have In Common
  - The Problem With Pride

- **Chapter Two**   13
  - Cain's Relationship To Abel
  - Abel's Relationship To God
  - God's Relationship to Cain
  - Did God Overreact?
  - The Problem With Jealousy

- **Chapter Three**   21
  - The Man That Didn't See Death
  - Enoch Really God's Friend?
  - Devoting Yourself To God

- **Chapter Four**   27
  - The Promises Of God
  - The Relationship Of God And Abraham
  - Sodom And Gomorrah
  - Abraham Makes The Rules
  - Lot Becomes An Example

- **Chapter Five**   39
  - The People God Chooses
  - David And Goliath
  - David And Bathsheba
  - What Made David So Special?

- **Chapter Six**   **57**
    - The Devil Is In The Details
    - The People Pleasers
    - Religious Extortion
    - Holier Than Thou
    - Religion vs. Relationship
    - Killing In The Name Of God
    - What Can We Do To Fix Things?

- **Chapter Seven**   **73**
    - Step One: Recognition
    - Step Two: Decision
    - Step Three: Forgiveness
    - Step Four: Have Faith
    - Step Five: Conversations With God
        - Why Doesn't God Answer My Prayers?
        - Can I Pray For Things I Want?
    - Step Six: Resistance
        - Soldiers In The Army Of God
    - Step Seven: Praising God

- **Chapter Eight**   **95**
    - The Human Body
    - Creativity
    - Desire For Knowledge
    - Jealousy
    - Anger
    - Sarcasm
    - Loving
    - Sense Of Humor
    - Forgiving
    - Sleep

- **Afterword - Sis. Taneka Dickson**   **a**
- **About The Author**   **c**
- **Post Reading Assessment Test**   **e**
- **Appendix A**
- **Appendix B**
- **Appendix C**

Acknowledgments

First and foremost, I would like to thank my Lord and Savior Jesus of Nazareth. This book was long overdue, and I couldn't have completed it without the inspiration and guidance of the Holy Spirit, the encouragement, dedication, help, and support of the following people: My parents, Pastor Perryetta Lacy and Brian Lacy, my wife to be Jenelle Jackson, my brother Derrius Fortson, my other brother Stanford Greenlee, my good friend Jenny Sampson, and last but certainly not least, Taneka Dickson.

I would also like to acknowledge the entire congregation of Ignited Praise Fellowship, all of which have been supportive of me in the ministry. Most of all, I would like to thank everybody who sat through my first few sermons without leaving. LOL (yes, I did that in a book).

I would like to thank Sis. Toni Terrell at The Answer for submitting my articles for publishing. You don't know how much I appreciate it. As I'm learning, it can be hard as a new minister to get people to take you seriously, but you made it so much easier.

Finally, I'd like to thank everyone reading this book, whether you bought it, borrowed it, or stole it (hopefully you didn't steal it). Thanks for your love and continued support. May God bless each and every one of you.

If there is anyone I forgot to mention by name, feel free to yell at me about it later, and I'll make sure to thank you on the website. I definitely don't want to leave out any important people.

How To Use This Book

As a life long reader and having a slight case of OCD when it comes to small things, I've arranged this book in a manner that I find to be least annoying to myself, so I apologize in advance if it feels a little different at first.

This book is meant to be a life long study, reference, and evaluation guide, as to where you are in your relationship with God. I tried to make things as easy to find and recognizable as possible because I hate to search through long blocks of text with no breaks.

I've tried to separate the content into as many sections as possible to allow you to find points of interest, quickly and easily. Another feature for those of you who hate to bend your pages or can't readily find a bookmark, I've included checkboxes on the Table Of Contents page, to allow you to keep track of where you are, by both chapter and section. If you don't like to write in your book, feel free to bend the page or use a bookmark. If you don't like to bend your pages, don't have a bookmark, and can't find a pen, just try not to have a panic attack, I'll pray for you to find one or the other.

> ❖ **Bible Verses** - All verses come from the King James Version of the Bible, and can be identified by the icon next to the verse.

> ➤ **Point To Ponder** - These are comments and questions that are designed to get you to think about the information that was just presented.

> o **Chapters Of Interest** - These are chapters and verses from the Bible that you may want to read in order to help you get a better understanding of the information that was just presented.

I also want to encourage you to check out every reference that I provide, and read every Chapter of Interest. Don't jus take my word for it. I'm human and I make mistakes.

After you finish reading Religion and Relationship, I also want to encourage you to go to my website and leave your comments and opinions on the book. I would appreciate you letting the world know how the book affected you personally.

Foreword

From the beginning, humanity has held a special place in the heart of God. Scripture tells us that we are on God's mind. David writes in Psalm 8:4: "What is man that thou are mindful of him or the son of man that thou visitest him (KJV)?" God actually thinks about us. David realized that the Creator truly contemplates His most treasured creation. There is a supernatural connection between God and man. It's so strong that it boggles the imagination, causes the angels to wonder and Satan to become jealous. After all, God the Son didn't lay down his life for Satan but for you and me. Now that's love.

In man's quest for connectedness with a power higher than himself, humanity has resorted to creating religious trappings that provide the feeling, sensation, and satisfaction of relationship but always comes short of true fulfillment. Over the course of time, man has resorted to worshipping the sun, moon, stars, trees, frogs, and even religion itself. Man continues to believe in and worship everything and everyone but God. In the name of religion, people have gotten so busy doing the Lord's work, they have forgotten about the Lord they are supposed to be working for. No wonder so many continue to miss Him.

Minister Dante Fortson candidly explores man's pursuit of the Almighty. He takes us on a journey from popular biblical figures to common religious practices, providing practical insights that point us back to right relationship with the Father, Son, and Holy Spirit.

This work has been a long time coming for Minister Dante, who had to revisit and recommit to his relationship with God, in order to achieve his supernatural purpose and occupy his divine destiny.

Thank you Minister Dante, for yielding yourself to be used by God and obediently walking in your calling. Lives will be absolutely changed because of your preaching, teaching, speaking and writing of the Word of God, because His Word will never, ever return void, incomplete, or unfulfilled, according to Isaiah 55.

Perryetta Lacy, MBA
Sr. Pastor of Ignited Praise Fellowship

Introduction

This book is the result of an extraordinary twenty-six year journey on this planet we call earth. I'm constantly amazed at how wonderful God is and how He uses the least likely people to accomplish His will. I realize that everything happens for a reason, and without the choices I made in the past, I may not be sitting here writing this book right now.

I personally believe that the Holy Spirit has inspired this book, and if you know me, then you know how big of a statement that is for me to make. In fact, you've probably never heard me say it before about anything. For those that don't know me, I am very careful about declaring things to be inspired by the Holy Spirit. I don't take God's work lightly, and I was even reluctant to do it from the very start.

I have always believed in God. I was saved and baptized at a very young age. I've never stopped believing in God, Jesus, The Holy Spirit, heaven, hell, angels, or demons, although I have strayed into various other belief systems and ideas. Don't misunderstand me, I have never switched or turned away from Christianity. My personal journey has been very long, even though I am only 26 years of age, it has consisted of Mysticism, New Age, aliens, UFOs, astral projection, NDEs, vampires, ghosts, channeling, etc. You name it, I've probably studied it or experienced it in ways that I shouldn't have.

I understand now that my entire life's journey has brought me to this new stage in my existence. I am now a licensed Minister and proud to be serving God's kingdom, as I should have been doing many years ago, but I ran the opposite direction even after I knew what I was supposed to be doing.

I can honestly say that my relationship with God didn't really develop until I went to jail December 19, 2008. I truly found God in jail because there isn't much to do while waiting for free time, except pray and read. Even in jail, one of my good friends, David Lee Hudson told me I was going to be a preacher, but I insisted that I would never preach a day in my life. I was content to just teach God's word in the background and maybe lead Bible study. Well, that wasn't in God's plan, and sure enough, not a full three months later, I preached my first sermon on how God chooses ordinary people to do extraordinary things. My next sermon was titled "Religion or

Relationship", which was soon followed by my next sermon, "What is Wrong With Your Relationship?"

I was only three sermons into my ministry when God chose to reveal to me His plans for a new generation of Christians. Christians that truly want to know Christ in a personal way and not just Christians that want to teach, preach, or sit on the pew every Sunday. I truly believe that the message in this book is the message that God has been trying to send us since the beginning. This is the message Christ was teaching the disciples as they walked and talked with Him.

The moment that led to me writing this book came just after my last sermon. Everything hit me all at once when it was revealed that God had used me to write a series of three related sermons that all touched on having a true relationship with Him. In all, it has taken me four weeks to complete the first draft of this book, and I estimate another two to three weeks worth of editing. In less than six months, the Lord has taken me from inmate to Minister to published author.

I believe this book transcends Christian denominations and focuses on having a true relationship with our Lord and Savior, Jesus Christ. Everyone will find something for them in this book, from the Atheist to the Pastor in the pulpit, from the thief to the murderer. The Holy Spirit has revealed to me just one of the many messages that God has been trying to get across to mankind since the beginning. My hope is that after you finish reading Religion and Relationship, you will either begin or renew your relationship with the Lord, Jesus Christ.

Throughout the Bible, God chooses men and women to carry out His will, take His message to the people, warn the world of things to come, and to be a witness to an unbelieving world. The Lord, walked, talked, and ate with a select few in both the Old and New Testaments, but why did He choose the people He did?

God doesn't use the type of people we think He should be using. Jesus doesn't hang out with the Scribes, Pharisees, and Sadducees, but instead chooses to associate Himself with the spiritual outcasts. Time after time in the scripture, we read about God working through people that don't fit the human idea of a person worthy of talking to God.

As you read through the Bible, you start to get the idea that God is "down to earth" in a manner of speaking. He's not as distant as He seems, and maybe He really does just want us to get to know Him. He agrees to play by Abraham's rules, He wrestles with Jacob, and He talks to Moses face to face. God wants to have that type of relationship with us all, but we have to meet Him half way.

Does God Really Want A Relationship?

God never has and never will abandon mankind. He has been trying to develop a personal relationship with mankind since He first placed man on the earth and put him in charge of all creation. Adam walked and talked with God in the Garden of Eden, Enoch walked with God before the flood, Abraham was called God's friend, and again, He talked to Moses, face to face.

We do not serve a Creator that can't relate to our struggle as humans, because He cared so much that He became human and subjected Himself to a death so horrific that most of us can't even imagine what it was really like. Christ laughed, cried, ate, drank, argued with the religious leaders, got angry, made wine, shared food, healed the sick, preached, prayed, taught, cast out demons, was born in a stable, lived on the street, had a bounty placed on Him as a baby, was baptized, mocked, rejected, loved, hated, beaten, killed, and resurrected, all for us. In some ways, Jesus almost seems more human than we could ever be.

Building On A Solid Foundation

Long before Catholics founded their religion on Peter, God was called the Rock. Moses and David both referred to the Savior and Rock of Israel, whom we know as Jesus Christ. What we believe needs to be established upon a firm foundation if our house of faith is going to stand up under pressure. In reference to our faith, Jesus said the following:

> ❖ "Whosoever cometh to me, and heareth my sayings, and doeth them, I will shew you to whom he is like: He is like a man which built an house, and digged deep, and laid the foundation on a rock: and when the flood arose, the stream beat vehemently upon that house, and could not shake

> it: for it was founded upon a rock. But he that heareth, and doeth not, is like a man that without a foundation built an house upon the earth; against which the stream did beat vehemently, and immediately it fell; and the ruin of that house was great." - Luke 6:47-49

Come along on this journey as we explore the will of God for mankind and the humanity of our Creator. I pray that this book will help you establish or re-establish your faith on the firm foundation of Jesus Christ, a foundation that can never be shaken or destroyed by anyone or anything.

Sincerely,

Minister Dante Fortson

> ❖ "Call unto me, and I will answer thee, and show thee great and mighty things which thou knowest not." - Jeremiah 33:3

Pre-Read Assessment Test

Testing Your Knowledge Of God

Please complete this short quiz before reading the book.

Do you believe God is forgiving?

- ❑ Yes
- ❑ No

Do you need to have your life in order before coming to God?

- ❑ Yes
- ❑ No

Does God help those that help themselves?

- ❑ Yes
- ❑ No

Does God prefer to use righteous people instead of sinners?

- ❑ Yes
- ❑ No

Is God still answering prayers?

- ❑ Yes
- ❑ No

Are you required to share your faith with others?

- ❑ Yes
- ❑ No

Does God expect us to be religious and follow church tradition?

- ❑ Yes
- ❑ No

Are religion and having a relationship with God different?

- ❑ Yes
- ❑ No

Verses To Remember

"Through desire a man, having separated himself, seeketh and intermeddleth with all wisdom."

Proverbs 18:1

"Thine own wickedness shall correct thee, and thy backslidings shall reprove thee: know therefore and see that it is an evil thing and bitter, that thou hast forsaken the LORD thy God, and that my fear is not in thee, saith the Lord GOD of hosts"

Jeremiah 2:19

Chapter 1: God, The Devil, and Adam

Sometimes what is not written in the Bible is just as important as what is written. Most of us know the story of Adam and Eve, the serpent, and the Tree of the Knowledge of Good and Evil. By the time we reach Genesis 3, Lucifer has already fallen from heaven and has become an enemy or adversary to God, and has intentions of becoming the enemy of mankind. At this point, Lucifer inherits the title "Ha Satan", "the adversary", but this is not intended to be an in depth theological study on the origins of Satan, but to show the kind of relationship that he once had with God.

The Devil (accuser), which is a New Testament title for Lucifer, has a few things in common with Adam when it comes to their relationship with God. In both cases, God assumes a parental role, and punishes His children according to their sin. Adam was called God's son, as was Satan.

> ❖ "Which was the son of Enos, which was the son of Seth, which was the son of Adam, which was the son of God." - Luke 3:38

> ❖ "Now there was a day when the sons of God came to present themselves before the LORD, and Satan came also among them." - Job 1:6

The phrase "sons of God" in the Old Testament is always used to refer to angels, with the exception of Adam. We as Christians are not referred to as sons of God until the New Testament, through the death, burial, and resurrection of Christ.

> ❖ "But as many as received him, to them gave he power to become the sons of God, even to them that believe on his name:" - John 1:12

Before Adam came along, there was Lucifer and God. According to Ezekiel 38:15, Lucifer was created perfect and was perfect, until iniquity was found in him.

Iniquity: gross injustice or wickedness, a violation of right or duty; wicked act; sin.

Lucifer's duty was to serve and worship God, but Isaiah 14:13-14 tells us that he violated his duty by wanting to be worshiped. His rebellion led astray one-third of the angels in heaven.

> ❖ "And his tail drew the third part of the stars of heaven, and did cast them to the earth: and the dragon stood before the woman which was ready to be delivered, for to devour her child as soon as it was born." – Revelation 12:4

Lucifer's Relationship With Mankind

> ❖ "But let him that glorieth glory in this, that he understandeth and knoweth me, that I am the LORD which exercise lovingkindness, judgment, and righteousness, in the earth: for in these things I delight, saith the LORD." – Jeremiah 9:24

The older I've gotten, the more I've questioned why God would cast Lucifer into the Lake of Fire without giving him a second chance. Jeremiah clearly states that God exercises loving kindness, and sending Lucifer to the Lake of Fire for a first offense hardly seems loving and kind. Regardless of how we may feel about the Devil, God still loves him, and sometimes the Scripture fills in little bits and pieces as we draw nearer to God and His word.

Heaven is God's house, and as a son of God, Lucifer was subject to obeying the rules of the house. As we get older, some of us have experienced feeling that we no longer have to obey the rules of our parent's home. At that point, we usually have to make the decision to stay and follow the rules, or leave and make our own rules to an extent.

In all of my studying, God has always been a God of second chances, and in my spirit, I know that Lucifer had a second chance. His first punishment was that he had to move out of God's house. There was nothing more to the punishment, as far as we know, except being kicked out of heaven. However, as with any parent, God still allowed Lucifer to come and visit (Genesis 3, Job 1:6, 2:1). Some of you may find that hard to digest at the moment, but God's word will support my view, so I encourage you to keep reading.

Chapter 1

Adam's Punishment

Adam's fall and Lucifer's second punishment go hand in hand. Again, sometimes what is not written is just as important as what is written. Neither Adam nor Eve found the serpent to be a strange creature, and both of them seemed to be familiar with the serpent in the Garden. I believe that just as in Job chapters 1 and 2, Satan was allowed to stop by God's garden. If Lucifer wasn't allowed in, God's army of angels would have kept him out of the garden to begin with. Among which, was a flaming sword that turned in every direction, so there wasn't going to be any sneaking in.

> ❖ "So he drove out the man; and he placed at the east of the garden of Eden Cherubim, and a flaming sword which turned every way, to keep the way of the tree of life." - Genesis 3:24

When Lucifer convinced Eve to eat the fruit, he caused an unexpected chain reaction. I don't believe Lucifer's intentions were to bring the full wrath of God upon himself. That seems to be a miscalculation in his plan. It seems as though he was confident in his immortality and was trying to bring down mankind and get revenge on God all in one go. But when God started handing out punishments, as a parent does when their children are disobedient, Lucifer became subject to a second punishment.

Adam and Eve were to be kicked out of the Garden, just as Lucifer had been kicked out of heaven. Adam would now have to work for his food and Eve would have pain in childbirth. Lucifer's appearance was changed, and the serpent was cursed to crawl after the fall of man, so I'm sure it looked completely different in the garden, and not like the snakes we are used to seeing today.

God told Adam that he would die if he ate the fruit (Genesis 2:17), and the Devil knew that because he twisted God's word while talking to Eve (Genesis 3:1). What the Devil didn't know, is that by tricking Eve into committing "suicide" so to speak, he himself also committed suicide. As I said before, the Devil's original punishment was being kicked out of heaven, but in Genesis 3:15, God announces to the Devil that he would be at war with the seed of the woman (Christ), and his own head would eventually be crushed because of his actions.

Lucifer's Relationship With God

Lucifer started out as the top angel, a cherub, not just any cherub, but the main guy. Common sense tells us that he was very powerful, in fact, his army was only 1/3 the size of heaven's army and he still thought he had a chance of success with his rebellion. Throughout history, the person that challenges the king for his throne the majority of the time is usually the jealous son. Lucifer becomes envious of God's power and wants it for himself.

> ❖ "How art thou fallen from heaven, O Lucifer, son of the morning! how art thou cut down to the ground, which didst weaken the nations! For thou hast said in thine heart, I will ascend into heaven, I will exalt my throne above the stars of God: I will sit also upon the mount of the congregation, in the sides of the north: I will ascend above the heights of the clouds; I will be like the most High." Isaiah 14:12-14

Even after Lucifer rebelled, God didn't destroy him. After he deceives Eve, God reaches His boiling point, and responds to Lucifer's famous "five I wills" with "five I will's" of His own.

> ❖ "By the multitude of thy merchandise they have filled the midst of thee with violence, and thou hast sinned: therefore I will cast thee as profane out of the mountain of God: and I will destroy thee, O covering cherub, from the midst of the stones of fire. Thine heart was lifted up because of thy beauty, thou hast corrupted thy wisdom by reason of thy brightness: I will cast thee to the ground, I will lay thee before kings, that they may behold thee. Thou hast defiled thy sanctuaries by the multitude of thine iniquities, by the iniquity of thy traffick; therefore will I bring forth a fire from the midst of thee, it shall devour thee, and I will bring thee to ashes upon the earth in the sight of all them that behold thee." - Ezekiel 28:16-18

Adam and Eve's sin caused them to be separated from God, which made it necessary for the Messiah to be born. Lucifer's first sin of rebellion also caused him to be separated from God. According to Revelation 20:10, the Messiah will cast the Devil into the Lake of Fire, which is the second death. Had Lucifer not tricked Eve, there would have been no need for a Messiah to be born, the Devil's head would not have to be bruised in judgment, and neither would he be facing death in the Lake of Fire. A series of unfortunate events for both mankind and the Devil. We all suffer from sin because of his actions and Adam and Eve's decision to disobey.

What Adam and Satan Have In Common

As we can see in the story of the Fall of Mankind, God takes on the relationship role of a Father to both Adam and Satan. Adam takes on the relationship role of the good son, who is led astray by the bad and disobedient son, Satan.

Before the fall of Lucifer, God and Lucifer had a friendship, which is evident in how highly God speaks of Lucifer in Ezekiel. Disobedience changed their relationship.

> ❖ "Son of man, take up a lamentation upon the king of Tyrus, and say unto him, Thus saith the Lord GOD; Thou sealest up the sum, full of wisdom, and perfect in beauty. Thou hast been in Eden the garden of God; every precious stone was thy covering, the sardius, topaz, and the diamond, the beryl, the onyx, and the jasper, the sapphire, the emerald, and the carbuncle, and gold: the workmanship of thy tabrets and of thy pipes was prepared in thee in the day that thou wast created. Thou art the anointed cherub that covereth; and I have set thee so: thou wast upon the holy mountain of God; thou hast walked up and down in the midst of the stones of fire. Thou wast perfect in thy ways from the day that thou wast created, till iniquity was found in thee." - Ezekiel 28:12-15

God is talking to the power behind the king of Tyrus, Satan. Lucifer was better than perfect. "Thou sealest up the sum", says it all, when it comes to how God felt about him. He was in God's garden, he was perfect in beauty, he was on God's holy mountain, and walked in the midst of the stones of fire. He was also perfect "till" iniquity was found in him.

Likewise, before the fall of mankind, Adam and God took walks in the Garden together, and Adam was even allowed to name all of God's earthly creation. Disobedience also changed Adam's relationship with God.

Both sons of God disobeyed, and both were "kicked out of God's house." Adam and Eve messed up their relationship with God, but through the Messiah, mankind can repair their relationship with God. Whatever transpired between God and the Devil after the fall, Satan was not destroyed and did not face eternal damnation until he continued to bring down the rest of God's creation. God is a God of second chances and He wants us to restore our relationship with Him.

> ❖ "The Lord is not slack concerning his promise, as some men count slackness; but is longsuffering to us-ward, not willing that any should perish, but that all should come to repentance." 2 Peter 3:9

As we can see, God is indeed loving and long suffering toward His sons and daughters. It is evident in the fact that He didn't just destroy Lucifer after his first offense. This makes me wonder if Lucifer had the chance to restore his relationship with God, but simply refused to do so. The good news is, our relationship can be restored, but only if we don't continue to reject God's mercy, which is a second offense, if we do not ask to be forgiven, before we die.

Satan's relationship with mankind became that of a jealous and mean spirited older brother. He is constantly trying to get the little brother (mankind) in trouble with the Father, which will further separate us from God's grace. The Devil is fully aware of his final fate and he does everything in his power to get mankind to share in his punishment.

Jesus points out a few interesting things about the Pharisees which gives us a little bit of insight into what the Devil's intentions are toward mankind.

> ❖ "Ye are of your father the devil, and the lusts of your father ye will do. He was a murderer from the

> beginning, and abode not in the truth, because there is no truth in him. When he speaketh a lie, he speaketh of his own: for he is a liar, and the father of it." - John 8:44

> ❖ "But woe unto you, scribes and Pharisees, hypocrites! for ye shut up the kingdom of heaven against men: for ye neither go in yourselves, neither suffer ye them that are entering to go in." - Matthew 23:13

If the Pharisees and Sadducees were like their father the Devil, then we know that their intentions weren't good. The Devil can't get back into heaven, and he definitely doesn't want us to get into heaven in the first place.

The Problem With Pride

As you read through the Bible, you get the idea that God hates pride. Pride is what started this whole mess in the first place. We saw in Isaiah 14:12-14 how prideful Lucifer was before his fall. Proverbs also testifies to how God feels about pride.

> ❖ "When pride cometh, then cometh shame: but with the lowly is wisdom." - Proverbs 11:12

> ❖ "Pride goeth before destruction, and an haughty spirit before a fall." - Proverbs 16:18

> ❖ "A man's pride shall bring him low: but honour shall uphold the humble in spirit." - Proverbs 29:23

There is no reason for man to be prideful. Salvation does not come through any good deed that man can do. God purposely made salvation a free gift to all mankind, so that no one could brag about their good deeds being responsible for earning them their way into heaven.

> ❖ "For by grace are ye saved through faith; and that not of yourselves: it is the gift of God: Not of works, lest any man should boast. - Ephesians 2:8-9

Paul expounds on the subject of boasting in Romans because it is important to understand that everything we have and will have is a result of God's grace and mercy. Lucifer was beautiful and powerful because God created him that way, not because he attained it himself.

> ❖ "For all have sinned, and come short of the glory of God; Being justified freely by his grace through the redemption that is in Christ Jesus: Whom God hath set forth to be a propitiation through faith in his blood, to declare his righteousness for the remission of sins that are past, through the forbearance of God; To declare, I say, at this time his righteousness: that he might be just, and the justifier of him which believeth in Jesus. Where is boasting then? It is excluded. By what law? of works? Nay: but by the law of faith." - Romans 3:23-27

If pride is what causes us to fall, we need to figure out what causes us to be raised up by God. In order to find grace with God, we need to be humble. Humility is the exact opposite of pride.

> ❖ "Likewise, ye younger, submit yourselves unto the elder. Yea, all of you be subject one to another, and be clothed with humility: for God resisteth the proud, and giveth grace to the humble." - 1 Peter 5:5

God resists the proud and gives grace to the humble. When we are prideful, we are putting ourselves in direct opposition with God, just as Lucifer did. When God told Solomon that he could ask for anything he wanted, Solomon was humble and asked God for the wisdom to lead God's people. Solomon himself testifies to this in Proverbs.

> ❖ "By humility and the fear of the LORD are riches, and honour, and life." - Proverbs 22:4

When the Bible speaks of fear, it is also referring to, as my mom puts it, a healthy respect of God. We may fear God's power, but we also need to respect who God is and what He does. Solomon had a healthy respect for God, just as his father

David did, that's why Solomon was already wise enough to realize he needed more wisdom. As a result, God gave him riches beyond belief, honor as a king, and long life.

> ❖ "The fear of the LORD is the beginning of wisdom: and the knowledge of the holy is understanding." - Proverbs 9:10

For those of us who insist on being prideful, Proverbs puts it in clear perspective once again.

> ❖ "Before destruction the heart of man is haughty, and before honour is humility." - Proverbs 18:12

The reason I'm trying to drive this point home is because pride is a huge problem in church, of all places. We have those people that think that because they are the head of all the church functions or make every Bible study, that they are some how above everyone else. We also have those that talk about all the "good" they do, but never mention their faults. We are human, and as a result, we tend to forget things, and one of those things is that Lucifer was PERFECT just before he rebelled against God. The Bible doesn't say that he thought he was perfect, it says he was perfect.

As Christians, we need to approach God's throne humbly when we pray, and be sure to give God the credit for everything we do. Some of us would like to believe we make things happen, but the truth is, we don't.

> ❖ "See now that I, even I, am he, and there is no god with me: I kill, and I make alive; I wound, and I heal: neither is there any that can deliver out of my hand." - Deuteronomy 32:39

Although God is a loving God that loves His creations, He hates the sins that we commit. God loves Lucifer, but He hates his pride, arrogance, and disobedience. God loved Adam and loves all mankind, but at times, we have the same problem Lucifer had, pride, arrogance, and disobedience. Those three things separated Lucifer from God and it threatens to separate us from God as well.

What Should We Take From This?

- God offers everyone at least two chances before they are sentenced to an eternal judgment.

- 1st Offense - Sinning against God.

- 2nd Offense - Rejecting God's mercy.

- God hates pride.

- We have no reason to be prideful.

- A healthy respect for God leads to humility.

- Humility leads to wisdom.

- Wisdom leads to long life, riches, and honor.

Chapters Of Interest

- Genesis 2
- Genesis 3
- Proverbs (The Entire Book)
- Ecclesiastes (The Entire Book)

Verses To Remember

"It is the glory of God to conceal a thing: but the honour of kings is to search out a matter."

Proverbs 25:2

"Thus saith the LORD, Let not the wise man glory in his wisdom, neither let the mighty man glory in his might, let not the rich man glory in his riches: But let him that glorieth glory in this, that he understandeth and knoweth me, that I am the LORD which exercise lovingkindness, judgment, and righteousness, in the earth: for in these things I delight, saith the LORD."

Jeremiah 9:23-24

Chapter 2: Relationship Lessons From Cain

In Genesis 4, we find the story of Cain and Abel. We don't know a whole lot about Cain and Abel. We have no idea how old they are in the story, and no idea what their relationship was like based on the text.

This story, even though its short, would make a great movie. We have sibling rivalry, deception, murder, punishment, and forgiveness; all the things that make a story interesting.

Cain's Relationship To Abel

Cain and Abel were brothers, as most of us already know. Throughout the Bible, God usually shows the younger brother favor over the older brother, which is the complete opposite of man's tradition.

> ❖ "And in process of time it came to pass, that Cain brought of the fruit of the ground an offering unto the LORD. And Abel, he also brought of the firstlings of his flock and of the fat thereof. And the LORD had respect unto Abel and to his offering: But unto Cain and to his offering he had not respect. And Cain was very wroth, and his countenance fell." – Genesis 4:3-5

Both Cain and Abel offered a sacrifice to God, but God only accepted Abel's. For the sake of topic, I will not go into the reasons why Abel's sacrifice was accepted and Cain's rejected, just yet.

> ❖ "And Cain talked with Abel his brother: and it came to pass, when they were in the field, that Cain rose up against Abel his brother, and slew him." – Genesis 4:8

Cain became jealous of Abel and killed him. Cain's relationship to Abel didn't seem to be that of a loving older brother.

Abel's Relationship To God

Abel raised sheep (Genesis 4:2), and he brought the first of his sheep as a sacrifice to God. By this single action, we know that God was first in Abel's life, and that seemed to please God. Because he pleased God, his sacrifice was accepted.

> ❖ "By faith Abel offered unto God a more excellent sacrifice than Cain, by which he obtained witness that he was righteous, God testifying of his gifts: and by it he being dead yet speaketh." - Hebrews 11:4

Because Abel had faith and he was obedient, his testimony still speaks to us today, even though he is long gone in his earthly form. Our hope should be that our actions through faith will testify to generations to come.

God's Relationship To Cain

After his sacrifice was rejected Cain's feelings were hurt. God offers consoling words to Cain, telling him that if he does right, his offering would be accepted, and Abel would be subject to him (Genesis 4:7). Because Cain did wrong, the roles were reversed and the elder ended up beneath the younger.

I feel it is very important to address many assumptions that come from this story. Scripture does not support some of the stories and speculations on Cain's relationship to God, but they are ideas created by men to fit certain theories they create themselves. Let's look at a few:

1. The Antichrist comes from Cain's line.
2. Cain's lineage is cursed.
3. Cain loses God's favor.

The belief that the Antichrist comes from Cain's line runs into a major problem when we get to Noah's flood in Genesis 6. How did Cain's lineage survive? Cain's punishment also gives rise to the unfounded theory that Seth's (the new son born in Abel's place) line is somehow righteous, but Cain's line is unrighteous. Again, Noah's flood presents a small problem because Seth's line was wiped out too with the exception of Noah. God curses Cain but there is no mention that his lineage is cursed. Not only does Cain not lose God's favor, but God places His divine protection over him and promises to take sevenfold vengeance on anyone that touches him.

Chapter 2

Did God Overreact?

As a result of Cain's actions, God places a curse on him, which Cain says, is too much for him to bear (Genesis 4:11-12). This prompts Cain to beg for God's mercy, and God gives it to him. When most people teach on Cain's curse, they fail to mention that God forgives Cain because Cain wholeheartedly repented.

> ❖ "And the Lord said unto him, Therefore whosoever slayeth Cain, vengeance shall be taken on him sevenfold. And the Lord set a mark upon Cain, lest any finding him should kill him." Genesis 4:15

Whatever mark was set upon Cain was not the result of the curse, but the result of God's grace, mercy, and protection. Cain was simply punished for his sin, just as his father Adam was. Cain was no different than any of us. His relationship with God shows that we can be forgiven by coming to God, acknowledging our offense, and seeking His forgiveness.

The Devil and Cain both received a harsh reaction from God when they took hostile actions toward His creation. God will not tolerate the destruction of His creation by angels or mankind.

> ❖ "Keep thee far from a false matter; and the innocent and righteous slay thou not: for I will not justify the wicked." - Exodus 23:7

And again, the scripture testifies to this:

> ❖ "These six things doth the LORD hate: yea, seven are an abomination unto him: A proud look, a lying tongue, and hands that shed innocent blood, an heart that deviseth wicked imaginations, feet that be swift in running to mischief, a false witness that speaketh lies, and he that soweth discord among brethren." - Proverbs 6:16-19

Pride, lies, and shedding innocent blood are the first three mentioned. Both the Devil and Cain were prideful. The Devil wanted to be worshiped, and Cain's pride was hurt when his offering was rejected, but Cain swallowed his pride and asked to be forgiven.

Both Cain and the Devil acted in a deceptive manner in order to harm God's creation. Satan lied to Eve about the tree, and Cain led his brother into the field under the false premise of conversation.

Satan, through his deception, killed Adam and Eve by convincing them to disobey God. Adam, Eve, and Abel were all innocent in God's eyes before they were killed, as a result of pride and jealousy.

The Problem With Jealousy

The Devil was jealous of God's love for mankind, which is part of the reason that he plotted to deceive Eve. Jealousy usually fuels an angered or hostile response from the person who is jealous. The most common reasons for jealousy are relationships and lack of recognition. You may get jealous if your husband or wife is getting attention from someone of the opposite sex. Jealousy over recognition is subtle in the fact that most people don't even think about it. You may get passed over for a promotion or an award that you feel should have gone to you and not the person that received it. Jealousy is a dangerous thing, and has led to the death of many people throughout history. Cain was jealous that God accepted Abel's sacrifice, but not his, and as a result, he killed Abel.

> ❖ "For jealousy is the rage of a man: therefore he will not spare in the day of vengeance." - Proverbs 6:34

Some of us would be surprised to learn that jealousy is not just a human trait, but a spiritual one as well. Satan was jealous of God's power and authority, so he coveted it for himself. God gets jealous when we worship anyone or anything but Him.

> ❖ "Ye shall not go after other gods, of the gods of the people which are round about you; (For the LORD thy God is a jealous God among you) lest the anger of the LORD thy God be kindled against thee, and

> destroy thee from off the face of the earth." - Deuteronomy 6:14-15

The Bible doesn't condemn jealousy, but it does offer a stern warning against its results. Jealousy is not a sin, but the actions you take from the result of your jealousy, can lead to sin. We see in 2 Corinthians that Paul is jealous over the church because he doesn't want them running after other gods. Paul's jealousy is much along the lines of God's jealousy toward us worshiping other gods.

> ❖ "For I am jealous over you with godly jealousy: for I have espoused you to one husband, that I may present you as a chaste virgin to Christ." - 2 Corinthians 11:2

What Should We Take Away From This?

- God forgives our sins if we acknowledge them and repent.

- God offers grace and mercy to those that repent of their sins.

- Jealousy can lead to sin, so we need to be mindful of what we get jealous about, and how we react to that jealousy.

Chapters Of Interest

- Genesis 4

Verses To Remember

"A wise man will hear, and will increase learning; and a man of understanding shall attain unto wise counsels:"

Proverbs 1:5

"Woe be unto the pastors that destroy and scatter the sheep of my pasture! saith the LORD."

Jeremiah 23:1

Chapter 3: The Man That Walked With God

In Genesis 5:19, we are introduced to a man by the name of Enoch. Next to Melchizedek, Enoch is probably one of the most mysterious characters in the Bible. Various works have surfaced, that claim to be written by this mysterious man in the Bible. However, most of what we know about Enoch comes from only a few verses in the Bible.

Enoch walked with God (Genesis 5:24), just before the flood of Noah. Up until Enoch, the only man that had been recorded as walking with God was Adam. This implies that there was something special about Enoch that allowed him to have a very close relationship with God.

The Man That Didn't See Death

Enoch was special because he "pleased God" according to Hebrews 11:5. God doesn't have many "friends" in the Bible, but I'll venture out on a limb and say Enoch was one of them.

The reason I feel comfortable making the statement that Enoch was God's friend, is because God and Enoch walked and talked together. When I say talked, I mean they literally talked, as you would with a close friend.

We know that Enoch talked with God, because Enoch was a prophet. In fact, he is the very first prophet recorded in the Bible, and I venture to say, the very first evangelist. We know that Enoch was a prophet because Jude 1:14 tells us that Enoch "prophesied".

For those that might not be comfortable with the idea the Enoch was the first evangelist, let me make you a little more uncomfortable, and go as far as to say that he was the first Christian. We know for certain that Enoch believed in the Messiah, because of the message he preached.

> ❖ "And Enoch also, the seventh from Adam, prophesied of these, saying, Behold, the Lord cometh with ten thousands of his saints, to execute judgment upon all, and to convince all that are ungodly among them of all their ungodly deeds which they have ungodly committed, and of all their hard speeches which ungodly sinners have spoken against him." – Jude 1:14-15.

Enoch preached a message of the Lord's return with His saints to judge the world, even though the Messiah had yet to be born, which brings us back to Hebrews 11:5.

It was Enoch's faith in God's word that allowed him to be translated, caught up, or raptured, just as all believers will be, according to 1 Thessalonians 4:17. God used Enoch's life as an example to all future followers of Christ.

As Christians or followers of Christ, we are told to preach the Good News (Gospel) to everyone (Mark 1:15), which Enoch did. We are also told that faith without works is dead (James 2:26), but Enoch took action by not only believing what God said, but by sharing the message that God had given him. Because Enoch was obedient to God, he was spared from the moment of tribulation (the flood), which came upon the entire world (Revelation 3:10).

Our current society is facing a similar situation. We have Christians preaching the good news of Christ return and the coming judgment. We also believe that just before that judgment Christ will remove believers, just as Enoch was removed before the flood. Sometimes we need to look just a little bit deeper than the surface to get the full message that God is sending.

Was Enoch Really God's Friend?

Jesus said that He only does what He sees the Father do (John 5:19). When He spoke with the disciples, He called them friends, simply because He was sharing with them what was going to happen in both the near and distant future (John 15:15). Even though he didn't live to see Christ coming with His saints, Enoch believed God, and as we will see later, our faith is counted as righteousness.

It's clear by Enoch's testimony that God shared with Enoch what was going to happen in the distant future. According to the scripture, Enoch would be considered a friend of God. As a result of his walk with God, Enoch became the very first friend of God recorded in the Bible, the first prophet, the first evangelist, and the first man to be caught up to heaven without dying. All these are promises that we as Christians have, through our relationship with Christ.

Chapter 3

Devoting Yourself To God

The Bible doesn't say much about what Enoch had, but we do know that Enoch devoted himself to God. He preached God's word and he walked with God. Based on that, I make the assumption that he also devoted everything else he had to God.

> ❖ "Notwithstanding no devoted thing, that a man shall devote unto the LORD of all that he hath, both of man and beast, and of the field of his possession, shall be sold or redeemed: every devoted thing is most holy unto the LORD." - Leviticus 27:28

Because Enoch devoted himself and all he had, he wasn't just considered holy, but "most holy" to God. Through his unwavering devotion to God, he was blessed that he didn't have to experience death.

What Should We Take From This?

- When we walk with God, our relationship changes from servant to friend.

- Completely devoting ourselves to God makes us most holy in His eyes.

Chapters Of Interest

- Genesis 5
- Hebrews 11
- Jude 1

Verses To Remember

"The fear of the LORD is the beginning of knowledge: but fools despise wisdom and instruction."

Proverbs 1:7

"For I know the thoughts that I think toward you, saith the LORD, thoughts of peace, and not of evil, to give you an expected end. Then shall ye call upon me, and ye shall go and pray unto me, and I will hearken unto you. And ye shall seek me, and find me, when ye shall search for me with all your heart. And I will be found of you, saith the LORD: and I will turn away your captivity, and I will gather you from all the nations, and from all the places whither I have driven you, saith the LORD; and I will bring you again into the place whence I caused you to be carried away captive."

Jeremiah 29:11-14

Chapter 4: Abraham Was A Friend Of God

In Genesis 11:29-32, we are introduced to a man named Abram, who will later be renamed Abraham. For some reason, God saw fit to select him out of everyone else on the planet. The Bible doesn't give us any specifics on why he was chosen, but there was something special about him.

You're going to hear me say it over and over again; sometimes what isn't written is just as important as what is written. Chapter 12 begins with God making seven promises to Abraham:

1. I will make you a great nation.
2. I will bless you.
3. I will make your name great.
4. You will be a blessing.
5. I will bless those that bless you.
6. I will curse those that curse you.
7. Everyone on earth will be blessed because of you.

What isn't written is how God and Abraham got to this point in their relationship. My personal opinion is that God and Abraham were already friends. I'm led to believe that they were friends because Abraham was 75 years old when he left home, there was no conversation that took place, Abraham didn't ask who God was, which was the opposite of what Moses did at the burning bush. He just grabbed his wife, he nephew Lot, and left his home. Abraham acted on his faith in God.

The Promises Of God

The seven promises that God makes to Abraham at the beginning of Genesis 12, are the foundational promises upon which all other promises to the nation of Israel are based.

I would also like to point out that these promises weren't made under any conditions. The Bible doesn't record Abraham having to do anything to receive these promises. God simply told him what He was going to do and He has continued to do it regardless of what the nation of Israel does.

> ❖ "And the scripture was fulfilled which saith, Abraham believed God, and it was imputed unto him for righteousness: and he was called the Friend of God." - James 2:23

If this book were about faith, I'd love to get into everything that Abraham did that showed his faith, but for now, we're going to stick to the relationship that God had with Abraham.

The Relationship Of God and Abraham

James 2:23 tells us that Abraham was called "the friend of God". Once again, I am led to return to the words of Jesus to the disciples.

> ❖ "Henceforth I call you not servants; for the servant knoweth not what his lord doeth: but I have called you friends; for all things that I have heard of my Father I have made known unto you." - John 15:15

God let Abraham in on a lot of information. Information that He really didn't have to share, but chose too because they were friends. Lets take a look at one specific event in Abraham and God's relationship. This event was the very first of its kind and revealed a different side of God that had not previously been seen in scripture.

Sodom and Gomorrah

Most of us are aware of the story of Sodom and Gomorrah, but what a lot of people aren't aware of, is the story that takes place prior to the main event. Abraham was living in the plains of Mamre and the Lord showed up with two angels. This story has plenty of significance, so lets break it down into minor details.

1. Abraham recognized the Lord and bowed to Him. This leads me to believe that this may not have been the first time the Lord dropped by. Its not recorded in the Bible that God visited Abraham on occasion, but its possible that is the reason he recognized Him.

2. Abraham requests that the Lord hangs out for a while to eat with him. The Lord agrees to Abraham's request.

3. The Lord asks where Sarah is and then tells Abraham that she is going to have a child.

4. Abraham walks and talks with the Lord and the angels on the way to Sodom. The Lord wonders if He should let Abraham in on His plans, but decides to do so based on their friendship. The two angels continue walking and leave Abraham and the Lord to their own private conversation.

5. Once the Lord fills Abraham in on the details, Abraham makes a statement that reveals that not only is he talking to God, but he is talking to God the Son, Jesus Christ before He becomes flesh in the New Testament.

> ❖ "That be far from thee to do after this manner, to slay the righteous with the wicked: and that the righteous should be as the wicked, that be far from thee: Shall not the Judge of all the earth do right?"
> - Genesis 18:25

We know this is Christ because Revelation 19:11 calls Christ is the righteous Judge of all the earth. Now that we know whom Abraham is talking to, the story starts to get a little more interesting.

Abraham Makes The Rules

Abraham had an ongoing friendship with the Lord. When Abraham saw Him approach, he immediately recognized his Friend, and welcomed Him to stay and eat.

In Matthew 16:16-17, when Peter recognized that Jesus was the Lord, Jesus told him, "my Father which is in heaven has revealed this to you". In the light of the New Testament, we now know that at some point, it was revealed to Abraham who Christ was.

Not only did Abraham know who He was, he also knew that the Lord would eventually judge the earth. With this in mind, Abraham began to ask his friend for a favor. Simply by asking, the Lord allowed Abraham to set the terms of their agreement.

> ➢ **Point To Ponder:** Just stop and think for a few seconds how close of a relationship Abraham had with the Lord. The Lord let Abraham set the terms of their agreement.

> ❖ "Declaring the end from the beginning, and from ancient times the things that are not yet done, saying, My counsel shall stand, and I will do all my pleasure:" - Isaiah 46:10

God can do anything He wants, but His relationship was so close with Abraham, that He not only considered Abraham's terms and conditions, He agreed to abide by them. Abraham asked the Lord to spare the city if there were at least ten righteous people in the city, but there weren't.

Why Was Abraham So Special?

The answer is a very simple one; Abraham believed and obeyed God. Belief and obedience are essential in a personal relationship with God. If we believe God, then obedience to God should come natural to us.

> ❖ "For what saith the scripture? Abraham believed God, and it was counted unto him for righteousness." - Romans 4:3

Abraham had unwavering faith that God would keep His promises and He has. Hebrews 11 is a perfect place to learn about the key components to Abraham's relationship with God.

> ❖ "By faith Abraham, when he was tried, offered up Isaac: and he that had received the promises offered up his only begotten son, Of whom it was said, That in Isaac shall thy seed be called: Accounting that God was able to raise him up, even from the dead; from whence also he received him in a figure." - Hebrews 11:17-19

Abraham had the kind of faith most of us only dreamed of having. He left his home based solely on the promises of God, then after God delivered on His promise to give him a son, God told him to Go sacrifice Isaac. At that very moment, Isaac was as good as dead, as far as Abraham was concerned.

On the surface, it seems like an odd request from God, but the scripture tells us that Abraham believed that God would resurrect Isaac from the dead. Abraham believed this because God told him that his seed would come through Isaac.

It took Abraham and Isaac three days to walk to the alter where he was supposed to be sacrificed, so lets take a look at it from a prophetic perspective.

Isaac, Abraham's only son, as far as God was concerned, was dead to Abraham for three days, after which, Abraham believed God would resurrect him from the dead, and in a manner of speaking He did. When they get to the place of sacrifice, Abraham reassures Isaac that God would provide a lamb (Christ) for the sacrifice. By simply being obedient, Abraham and Isaac became a foreshadowing of things to come. Christ (the lamb), the only begotten of the Father, would be dead to God for three days, and would then be resurrected.

Lot Becomes An Example

Lot's story isn't as in depth as Abraham, but there are still a few things we know about Lot.

1. He was Abraham's nephew.
2. Lot and Abraham were very close.
3. Lot was righteous.
4. Lot set his own terms.
5. Lot escaped judgment.

Although the Lord allowed Abraham to set the terms, notice that he did not mention his nephew Lot when negotiating with the Lord. Lot and Abraham may have been so close because Lot was the son of Abraham's dead brother Haran. The Lord didn't find the 10 righteous men that Abraham negotiated for, but He still sent His angels into the city on a search and rescue mission, partially as a favor to His friend, but definitely as a sign to us as believers.

> ❖ "And turning the cities of Sodom and Gomorrah into ashes condemned them with an overthrow, making them an ensample unto those that after should live ungodly; And delivered just Lot, vexed with the filthy conversation of the wicked: (For that righteous man dwelling among them, in seeing and hearing, vexed his righteous soul from day to

> day with their unlawful deeds;) The Lord knoweth how to deliver the godly out of temptations, and to reserve the unjust unto the day of judgment to be punished:" - 2 Peter 2:6-9

When the angels reached Lot, they told him what was going to happen, and he believed them. Lot is old and doesn't think that he will make it as far as the angels ask him to go, so he requests that him and his family are allowed to run to the mountains in Zoar. We know that Abraham believed God and it was counted to him as righteousness, so it is safe to believe that Lot also believed God, and that is why he is referred to as righteous in 2 Peter 2:8.

Lot may or may not have known that he was going to be used as a foreshadowing of things to come. Either way, the fact the Abraham didn't mention Lot in his request is very important in shedding light on his relationship with God.

1. God knows them that are His (2 Timothy 2:19).
2. God does a lot more than we ask of Him (Ephesians 3:20).
3. God will not destroy the righteous with the wicked (1 Thessalonians 5:9)

These are all promises of God that were not revealed to mankind until after Christ's death, but both Lot and Abraham knew of these things, because they had a relationship with the Lord.

2 Peter 2:6 tells us that Sodom and Gomorrah was to be an example to people after that, who would still choose to live ungodly. Just before Lot and his daughters (the righteous), were taken from the city, there was a wide acceptance of open homosexuality. It had become normal practice, and everyone was "out of the closet".

> ❖ "But the men of Sodom were wicked and sinners before the LORD exceedingly." - Genesis 13:13

> ❖ "But before they lay down, the men of the city, even the men of Sodom, compassed the house round, both old and young, all the people from every quarter: And they called unto Lot, and said

> unto him, Where are the men which came in to thee this night? bring them out unto us, that we may know them. And Lot went out at the door unto them, and shut the door after him, And said, I pray you, brethren, do not so wickedly." - Genesis 19:4-7

The term "know" used here is a Hebrew word referring to intimacy. They didn't want to just meet the visitors because there is nothing wicked in getting to know someone. They wanted to have sex with the angels that had just come into town.

If we look around today, we can see what it may have looked like when it first started. We have gay pride parades, gay clubs, gay rights, and the list goes on and on. However, I don't think the homosexual sin in Sodom and Gomorrah was the only reason for its destruction, but just one thing among many others. 2 Peter 2:7 tells us that even their conversation was filthy. When God led Peter to write, we know that the purpose was to shed a little more light on the situation.

Again, lets look at modern society. In 1960 it was rare to find a T.V. show where the husband and wife slept in the same bed. It was considered taboo. I wasn't alive then, but I've seen plenty of shows from that time period. Now it's not unusual to see unmarried strangers having sex on primetime television. Softcore pornography is no longer confined to HBO and Cinemax. More and more bad language is being allowed on television and as a society we have slowly become desensitized to it. What use to be frowned upon is now accepted as normal without question.

God is telling us what to look for just before we get "caught up" to be with the Lord. We are called friends of God, and therefore God is telling us all things before they come to pass. We will be snatched away, rescued, and delivered to safety, just before the world is judged. The destruction of Sodom and Gomorrah began the same day that Lot left the city.

Jesus makes a statement to His disciples, and I believe, this verse, transcends both time and religion.

> ❖ "But these things have I told you, that when the time shall come, ye may remember that I told you of them. And these things I said not unto you at the beginning, because I was with you." - John 16:4

Most of us don't consider the full scope of Jesus' words at all times, when we read the Bible. Sometimes the Lord speaks in past, present, and future, all at the same time. Lets break down His statement.

> ❖ "But these things have I told you, that when the time shall come, ye may remember that I told you of them." - John 16:4

Here the Lord is reminding the disciples of what He has taught them, because sometime in the future they will need to remember those things. I also believe He is reminding mankind of things in the past that we need to remember. A lot of the time Jesus uses parables to get a point across. The story of Sodom and Gomorrah serves as a story and a prophetic forewarning. Remember, Christ went to warn Abraham just before Sodom and Gomorrah were destroyed.

Christ seems to be present just before almost every major event throughout the Bible. As we read, we encounter a strange character whom we refer to as the Angel of the Lord. He wouldn't be strange except that He never reveals His name and He refers to Himself as God. We see Him just before Abraham sacrifices Isaac. We see Him again in the burning bush just before Moses confronts Pharaoh. He appears again before Joshua destroys Jericho. He announces the birth of Samson. David mentions Him on several occasions. He appears to Joseph to tell him not to put away Mary. After that, He is not seen again until after the resurrection. And finally in Revelation in reference to Christ.

Lets not just speculate on who the angel of the Lord is because Jesus tells us that He is the angel of the Lord.

> ❖ "Jesus said unto them, Verily, verily, I say unto you, Before Abraham was, I am. Then took they up stones to cast at him: but Jesus hid himself, and went out of the temple, going through the midst of them, and so passed by." - John 8:58-59

Jesus referred to Himself as "I Am" which is the same name God gives to Moses at the burning bush. If we read Exodus 3:2 carefully, we see that it was the Angel of the Lord in the burning bush.

> ❖ "And these things I said not unto you at the beginning, because I was with you." - John 16:4

He is revealing these things, just as He prepares to be crucified. Jesus says He doesn't tell them previously because He was with them, but now that it is His time to go, He reveals everything plainly to the disciples.

In the Old Testament, the Lord directly and physically interacted with mankind through the person we know to be the Angel of the Lord. In the New Testament, the Word became flesh and dwelled among mankind. Now that He is no longer physically interacting with mankind, Christ felt it was important to remind us of things in the past.

Thanks to the Holy Spirit, working through the writers of the Bible, we can put together various signs of Christ's return for the Church, and the coming judgment on the world. Four of them we get from the story of Sodom and Gomorrah.

1. Filthy conversation becomes normal.
2. Homosexuality becomes widely accepted.
3. The righteous are warned before the coming judgment.
4. The righteous are removed before the judgment.

This is where the truth of God's Word transcends man's ideas and religious beliefs. Some of us are so caught up in pre-tribulation, mid-tribulation, post-tribulation, and pre-wrath rapture beliefs that we miss the point God is trying to make entirely. We won't endure the wrath of God regardless of when the rapture occurs.

Mankind and religion has put God into some sort of box, when God has refused to put Himself in a box. Based on the word of God, we know:

1. Whether we choose to believe in pre-tribulation, mid-tribulation, post-tribulation, or pre-wrath, we all agree the Christ is coming back for us.

2. No matter which position we take, we all believe that we will spend eternity with Christ.

If we are truly saved and covered by the blood of Christ, it really shouldn't matter when He returns for us. Prepare for the worst, but pray for the best. That may sound like a lack of faith, but it's quite the opposite. God answers all of our prayers, but sometimes we don't get the answer we think we want.

The rapture will occur on God's time and not a nanosecond before He is ready. All of us as Christians should be prepared to endure the Tribulation, but pray that we don't have to endure it.

Because Lot was righteous, the Lord used Lot to send a message to us, thousands of years in advance, in order to help us recognize those things that are already taking place. When you step out of the box of religion and into an open relationship with God, mysteries will be revealed to you.

What Should We Take From This?

- God reveals things to His friends.

- God listens to His friends.

- God keeps His promises to His friends.

- God will not punish His friends along with His enemies.

Chapters Of Interest

- Genesis 12
- Genesis 13
- Genesis 14
- Genesis 15
- Genesis 16
- Genesis 17
- Genesis 18
- Genesis 19

Verses To Remember

"How long, ye simple ones, will ye love simplicity? and the scorners delight in their scorning, and fools hate knowledge? Turn you at my reproof: behold, I will pour out my spirit unto you, I will make known my words unto you."

Proverbs 1:22-23

"Behold, I am the LORD, the God of all flesh: is there any thing too hard for me?"

Jeremiah 32:27

Chapter 5: The Company God Keeps

When I was growing up, occasionally, I would hear someone one say, "People judge you by the company you keep" and "God helps those who help themselves". As I got older, the second phrase made less sense to me because, if I could help myself, why would I need God's help? The Bible teaches a message that is in opposition to that line of thinking.

> ❖ "Unless the LORD had been my help, my soul had almost dwelt in silence." – Psalm 94:17

David knew he couldn't help himself at that point and even testifies that if the Lord weren't there he would have died. David was on the run from king Saul and there was nothing he could do, so he turned it all over to God.

> ➢ **Point To Ponder:** God helps those that realize they can't help themselves.

Let's get back to the first statement: "People judge you by the company you keep". That's a very interesting statement, but I wonder how many people have considered the kind of company God keeps, and how many of those people that believe that statement would apply that logic to God Himself.

This chapter, above all others, is very personal to me because of what I've been through, and I believe everyone will find someone they can relate to in the Bible. The message the Bible is sending, through the people God has chosen, is one of love and acceptance in spite of your past.

Throughout the Bible, God establishes a strange pattern when choosing people to do His will. The first time I started digging into this, I was very excited to see what kind of God we serve. Now more than ever before, I feel I have a better understanding of how God operates, and the message He has been trying to send us.

> ❖ "I am sought of them that asked not for me; I am found of them that sought me not: I said, Behold me, behold me, unto a nation that was not called by my name. I have spread out my hands all the day unto a rebellious people, which walketh in a

> way that was not good, after their own thoughts;" - Isaiah 65:1-2

God is making reference to Israel, but it also seems to apply to the individuals He has chosen to carry out His divine plan. Those of us He chooses, tend to be rebellious and dead set on having our own way and doing what we want to do, but God has other plans in mind.

Ever since God liberated Israel from Egypt, they have been in rebellion against Him, but He continues to show them grace and mercy because of the promises He made to Abraham, Isaac, and Jacob. God has not and will not forsake His chosen people.

The People God Chooses

Noah – We've all heard of Noah, the ark, the animals coming to the ship two by two, the flood that covers the earth, and the promise God makes to Noah after its all said and done. Sure, Noah did God's will, but what kind of man was Noah that God would choose him above all others? Although there were things that occurred in Genesis 6 that may have played a part in God choosing Noah, we know that Noah was an ordinary man, just like us.

> ❖ "These are the generations of Noah: Noah was a just man and perfect in is generations, and Noah walked with God." - Genesis 6:9

The Bible says Noah was "perfect in his generations", but that's not hard to be, when the world is so bad that God intends to wipe it out. Aside from that, the word used for perfect in Genesis 6:9 is a Hebrew word that refers to Noah's untainted DNA and not his moral Character. There were some strange things going on in Noah's day, and God needed to choose a man to keep the human race alive.

As we continue reading the story of Noah, we find out that Noah grew grapes and made wine; in other words, he owned a vineyard. I'm not sure if this was Noah's profession before the flood or something new he started after the flood, but Noah had quite a few drinks one night, and something strange happened between him and his younger son, which causes him to curse Canaan, his grandson.

> ❖ "And Noah awoke from his wine, and knew what his younger son had done unto him." – Genesis 9:24

When I was younger and my grandfather was still alive, we would plant a garden every year, and he also had different kinds of fruit trees. After the fruit was ripe, we would always go and pick it off the trees, and he would pull up whatever he planted in the garden. My point is that people that grow produce for a living or for personal use often partake in what they grow, and God already knew that Noah liked to drink. I say that because I'm pretty sure that wasn't his first drink and it may not have been his last, but my assumption is that Noah may have been what we call, an alcoholic.

Regardless of Noah's tendency to drink, God still chose him to be the one to preserve mankind and the rest of creation, when He asked Noah to build the ark. Noah was blessed because he obeyed God, not because he was so much better than anyone else.

Abraham – When we read the story of Abram and Sarah in Sunday school or Bible study, we often pay more attention to how faithful Abraham was and how he obeyed God. What is often glanced over, are the few times Abraham engaged in practices, that today, are considered, out of the ordinary to say the least.

> ❖ "And Abram was very rich in cattle, in silver, and in gold." – Genesis 13:2

The Bible tells us that Abraham was a very rich man, but how did Abraham get rich? The Bible doesn't mention how rich Abraham was until after he leaves Egypt. So now the question that you should be asking is, what did Abraham do in Egypt that made him so rich?

Abraham was worried that he would be killed because his wife was so beautiful, so he told her to lie and say that she was his sister. The princes of Egypt must have thought she was gorgeous too, because they took her to Pharaoh, and he gave Abraham "sheep, oxen, asses, menservants, maidservants, she asses, and camels" (Genesis 12:16). Sarah must have looked pretty good for Abraham to get all of that from the king of Egypt.

What would we call what Abraham did, in our day and age? We call it pimping. Yes, that may shock you, but lets be real about it. When a man convinces a woman to exchange her body for profit, for his own personal benefit, we usually refer to him as a pimp, (unless your in Las Vegas, and its an escort company, we call them businessmen).

Abraham may have done it out of fear, but he still did it, not once, but twice. The first time, the Bible makes no mention that Pharaoh didn't have sex with Sarah, but the second time Abraham and Sarah deceive Abimelech, God keeps Abimelech from touching her, and he is blessed because of it (Genesis 20).

Let's compare the two stories. In story number one God plagues Pharaoh, but in story number two, God blesses Abimelech. God Himself says He kept Abimelech from touching her, but there is no mention of that with Pharaoh. Abraham feared for his life, but did it bother him that another man was having sex with his wife? After all, the Bible never records him speaking to Sarah about it after the fact.

Something more interesting than any of that is the fact that God doesn't chastise Abraham about loaning out his wife or later having sex with Hagar to conceive Ishmael. In fact, God blesses one of the men Abraham loans his wife to, consoles Hagar, and promises to make Ishmael a great nation.

Lot – Most of us only know of Lot because of Sodom and Gomorrah. Other than that he isn't mentioned much. Lot turns out to be more important than some of us realize.

After Lot escapes from Sodom with his two daughters (his wife died), they end up in the mountains of Zoar. The older daughter devises a plan to get Lot drunk so she and her younger sister can have sex with their father in order to preserve mankind (Genesis 19:32). Lots older daughter assumed that the angels destroyed the whole world. Long story short, Lot gets drunk, has sex with his daughters, and they both end up pregnant. The Bible is more interesting than any soap opera you can put on television.

Why exactly is Lot such an important person? Lot is related to Jesus. Sometimes God definitely works in mysterious ways. So let's follow the bloodline briefly.

Lot's older daughter gives birth to Moab, the father of the Moabites. Fast forward to Ruth, who is a Moabitess. Ruth marries Boaz and gives birth to Obed. Obed has a son named Jesse and Jesse has a son named David, whom we know is related to Jesus. It's very interesting that God would use a man that had sex with his own daughters, to eventually bring about the birth of the Messiah.

Jacob - The majority of us know Jacob as Israel, the father of the twelve tribes of Israel. Before Jacob became the father of a great nation, he was a grifter, a thief, a conman, a scam artist, or whatever you want to call him.

Jacob started walking the fine line between opportunist and conman when he was very young. In Genesis 25:27-34, we find Esau exhausted, hungry, and thirsty to the point that he believed he is going to die. Jacob saw an opportunity to profit from Esau's predicament and made Esau sell him his birthright in exchange for food. Contrary to popular belief, this wasn't actually a scam. Esau wasn't thinking clearly, and made a bad judgment, but it was a fair trade. Esau thought the value of living was worth more than his birthright at that time (Genesis 25:32).

Many years later, when Isaac is old and about to die, Jacob's mother sees and opportunity to run a confidence scam on Isaac. If you don't know what a confidence scam is, its basically gaining someone's confidence by pretending to be someone you're not, in order to benefit from deceiving the other person.

To me, this wasn't an amateur scam that Jacob and his mother pulled. Rebekah came up with the idea, but Jacob found a hole in the plan. He knew he didn't smell or feel like Esau, so he told his mother that they might have a bit of a problem pulling it off. Jacob and Rebekah then conspire to pull of the biggest scam in human history. Rebekah cooks a goat just the way Isaac likes it, she puts the hair on Jacob so he feels and smells like Esau, and sends him in to Isaac with the food (Genesis 27:17).

Isaac, who is pretty much blind at this point, is suspicious, but the plan works, and Jacob receives the blessing that Isaac intends for Esau. The reason this blessing was so important, is because the receiver would be the one that all nations would eventually bow to, and the receiver would be the one through which the Messiah would eventually come. Jacob literally stole the Messianic line.

Eventually, Isaac, who is about to die, makes a last request of Jacob and asks that he marry one of Laban's daughters. Laban is also a conman, so the story starts to get a little more interesting at this point. Just imagine, two scam artists, both trying to out con the other one.

Jacob sees Rachel, his cousin, and it is love at first sight. Laban, who is Jacob's uncle and Rebekah's brother, agrees to let Jacob marry Rachel if he will work for seven years to "earn" her (Genesis 29:20). After Jacob completes his seven years of service to Laban, his uncle, he is tricked into marrying the older daughter Leah.

> ❖ "And it came to pass, that in the morning, behold, it was Leah: and he said to Laban, What is this thou hast done unto me? did not I serve with thee for Rachel? wherefore then hast thou beguiled me? And Laban said, It must not be so done in our country, to give the younger before the firstborn." - Genesis 29:25-26

At this point, I think it is important to point out just how dysfunctional this family really is. The younger brother (Jacob) uses the older brother's (Esau) moment of weakness to gain something for himself. The mother (Rebekah) and younger son (Jacob) conspired to deceive Isaac into giving Jacob Esau's blessing. Now Laban tricks his nephew (Jacob) into marrying his older cousin (Leah), and his younger daughter (Rachel) has to wait another seven years to marry the man she's in love with (Jacob). If that's not dysfunctional, I don't know what is.

Now Jacob has worked an additional seven years, and has married both of his cousins, but I'm guessing he was still just a

Chapter 5

tad bit upset over what has transpired over the last fourteen years of his life. Jacob sees how much God has blessed Laban and Jacob decides he wants a piece of the action.

Jacob tells Laban that he only wants the spotted, brown, striped, and blemished sheep, cattle, and goats, and Laban agrees to the terms (Genesis 30:32-33). Jacob, being the person he is, isn't going to leave anything up to chance, so he figures out how to get the sheep, cattle, and goats to only produce blemished offspring. Not only is he conning his way to wealth, but he is only breeding the weak livestock to produce for Laban, so all of Laban's livestock is feeble, while Jacob's remains strong (Genesis 30:42). I bet you're wondering how he pulled all that off right? God was in on it and told Jacob what to do in a dream (Genesis 31:11-13). This goes back to the promises God made to Abraham to bless those that bless him and curse those that curse him.

God knows from the beginning what kind of man Jacob will be, and yet He chose him anyway, in spite of his shortcomings and downfalls.

Joseph - I'm sure you're thinking that Joseph couldn't possibly have any skeletons in his closet according to the Bible, but Joseph wasn't squeaky clean by man's standards. Joseph was an innocent man that was wrongfully accused of attempting to rape Potiphar's wife.

> ❖ "And it came to pass about this time, that Joseph went into the house to do his business; and there was none of the men of the house there within. And she caught him by his garment, saying, Lie with me: and he left his garment in her hand, and fled, and got him out. And it came to pass, when she saw that he had left his garment in her hand, and was fled forth, That she called unto the men of her house, and spake unto them, saying, See, he hath brought in an Hebrew unto us to mock us; he came in unto me to lie with me, and I cried with a loud voice: And it came to pass, when he heard that I lifted up my voice and cried, that he left his garment with me, and fled, and got him out. And she laid up his garment by her, until his lord came home. And she spake unto him according to these

> words, saying, The Hebrew servant, which thou hast brought unto us, came in unto me to mock me: And it came to pass, as I lifted up my voice and cried, that he left his garment with me, and fled out. And it came to pass, when his master heard the words of his wife, which she spake unto him, saying, After this manner did thy servant to me; that his wrath was kindled. And Joseph's master took him, and put him into the prison, a place where the king's prisoners were bound: and he was there in the prison." - Genesis 39:11-20

Let's look at what would have happened in our modern justice system. Joseph would have a felony arrest showing on his record. He spent time in prison, so he would be a convicted felon, and finally he would have to register as a sex offender because he was convicted of the crime. Even though he was completely innocent the conviction would have been enough to label him as a sex offender.

Moses - This man led the nation of Israel out of captivity and to the edge of the Promised Land, but before he became a great prophet and savior of the Israelites, Moses had a few issues.

The first problem Moses had, was that he was a fugitive, wanted for murder. One day Moses saw an Egyptian beating on one of the Hebrew slaves, so he killed him and hid the body when he thought no one was looking, but it wasn't as much of a secret as he thought it was.

> ❖ "And he said, Who made thee a prince and a judge over us? intendest thou to kill me, as thou killedst the Egyptian? And Moses feared, and said, Surely this thing is known. Now when Pharaoh heard this thing, he sought to slay Moses. But Moses fled from the face of Pharaoh, and dwelt in the land of Midian: and he sat down by a well." - Exodus 2:14-15

While Moses is on the run, he becomes a shepherd, and one day he loses one of his sheep. As he is looking for the lost sheep, he sees a bush that's on fire, but not burning up (Exodus 3:2-3).

> ❖ "And the angel of the LORD appeared unto him in a flame of fire out of the midst of a bush: and he looked, and, behold, the bush burned with fire, and the bush was not consumed. And Moses said, I will now turn aside, and see this great sight, why the bush is not burnt." - Exodus 3:2-3

This is where we learn about Moses' final two problems. Number one, he stutters (Exodus 4:10), and number two, he tells God to find someone else (Exodus 4:13). God could have chosen anyone to do His work, but He chose a hard headed, stuttering, murdering, fugitive to free His people.

> ❖ "And the LORD spake unto Moses face to face, as a man speaketh unto his friend..." Exodus 33:11

David – King David is probably one of the greatest kings in history, and one of my most favorite people in the Bible. David is special for several reasons, and all of them show us just how human he was, and just how awesome the God we serve is.

David was the smallest of his brothers, and even Samuel, a prophet, was shocked that God chose him over his brothers. Even God, speaking through Samuel, to Saul, about David, said:

> ❖ "But now thy kingdom shall not continue: the LORD hath sought him a man after his own heart, and the LORD hath commanded him to be captain over his people, because thou hast not kept that which the LORD commanded thee." - 1 Samuel 13:4

> ➤ **Point To Ponder:** God called David a man after His own heart.

More than anything else, David loved God. As we progress, we'll start to see how important David's total devotion to God truly is. As humans, we sometimes want to blame God for anything bad that happens, but we rarely place the blame on our own decisions.

It's important to understand that David was chosen as a child, and as a child, David had "anger issues", but his anger issues came as a result of other people's actions toward God. Think back to Chapter One, when I told you God takes action when someone commits a hostile act toward His creation. Well, David moves into action when someone becomes hostile towards God's will. David had God's back, and God had David's back. They were true friends.

David and Goliath

Let's start with the story of Goliath. David wasn't originally in camp to fight Goliath, he was there to bring his brothers lunch. While he was delivering their lunch, he overheard Goliath being disrespectful toward God and the armies of Israel.

> ❖ "And the Philistine said, I defy the armies of Israel this day; give me a man, that we may fight together." - 1 Samuel 17:10

> ❖ "And as he talked with them, behold, there came up the champion, the Philistine of Gath, Goliath by name, out of the armies of the Philistines, and spake according to the same words: and David heard them." - 1 Samuel 17:23

> ❖ "Thy servant slew both the lion and the bear: and this uncircumcised Philistine shall be as one of them, seeing he hath defied the armies of the living God." - 1 Samuel 17:36

Again, let's not forget that David is still a kid at this point and the smallest of eight brothers, but his faith is huge. David believes that God will deliver Goliath into his hand, regardless of the odds. Even Saul, the king, didn't have faith in God's ability to deliver Goliath into David's hand.

> ❖ "And Saul said to David, Thou art not able to go against this Philistine to fight with him: for thou art but a youth, and he a man of war from his youth." - 1 Samuel 17:33

Saul was looking at the outward appearance, just like Samuel was doing before God chose David, and just as we still do today. Goliath was 9 ½ feet tall, and David wasn't even close to his height. David had the kind of relationship with God that allowed him to face a fully armored giant, with only a hand full of rocks. In fact, David chose exactly five smooth stones.

Why exactly is it important that David chose five stones? It's a testimony to David's faith. David wasn't afraid that he would miss, because he was walking in the Spirit. Goliath had four brothers, Ishbibenob (2 Samuel 21:16), Saph (2 Samuel 21:18), Sippai (1 Samuel 21:19)(1 Chronicles 20:4), and another unnamed giant (1 Samuel 21:20, 1 Chronicles 20:6). David had faith that God would only need one stone for each of the five giants.

> ❖ "These four were born to the giant in Gath, and fell by the hand of David, and by the hand of his servants." - 2 Samuel 21:22

David And Bathsheba

Aside from having anger issues when God was mocked, David had other shortcomings that got him into trouble. One day David saw a beautiful woman bathing, and he wanted her. The problem is that she was married to a man in his army.

David decided to sleep with the woman anyway, and she gets pregnant. He knows what he has done is wrong, and tries to trick the woman's husband into coming home and sleeping with his wife. It doesn't work, so David has the man killed, and takes Uriah's wife as his own.

As you can guess, God isn't pleased at all and David's son dies after his birth. But look at the reaction has to God letting his son die.

> ❖ "Then said his servants unto him, What thing is this that thou hast done? thou didst fast and weep for the child, while it was alive; but when the child was dead, thou didst rise and eat bread. And he said, While the child was yet alive, I fasted and wept: for I said, Who can tell whether GOD will be gracious to me, that the child may live? But now he is dead, wherefore should I fast? can I bring him back again? I shall go to him, but he shall not

> return to me. And David comforted Bathsheba his wife, and went in unto her, and lay with her: and she bare a son, and he called his name Solomon: and the LORD loved him." - 2 Samuel 12:21-24

David didn't get mad or blame God because he knew his actions were unrighteous. Once everything was made right, God blessed him with another child by the name of Solomon. Look at the chain reaction that takes place, all over lust.

> ❖ "Then when lust hath conceived, it bringeth forth sin: and sin, when it is finished, bringeth forth death." - James 1:15

What Made David So Special?

David experienced life to the fullest. He may have had regrets, but in the end, David led a very full life. Together, with God, he fought bears, lions, giants, and armies. He was the underdog. He loved those close to him and he lost those close to him. He danced naked in the street and he mourned in sackcloth. He had an affair, he stole another man's wife, and he had his wives stolen from him twice; once by king Saul and again by his very own son. His best friend was killed, he was hunted by men, he was a fugitive, he was a pursuer, he went from shepherd boy to king of a nation, he lost sons, and he adopted other people's kids.

Through everything he went through, David never lost sight of God, and he continued to trust that whatever happened, it was completely in God's control.

Daniel - Daniel was an Old Testament prophet that was given the most detailed vision of the future of mankind recorded in the Bible. While Revelation was vivid, Daniel saw the last four empires on earth, the rapture, the Antichrist, world war three, the sudden knowledge increase of the last days, the rapture, the resurrection of the dead, the second coming of Christ, and the final judgment.

Daniel was very wise, and may have seen a lot more than what was written in the book. This is indicated by the presence of the Magi when king Herod was trying to find where Christ was born. The Magi were a group of Persian wise men that were very important. The king asked them where the Messiah would be born because there was something special about them.

> ❖ "It pleased Darius to set over the kingdom an hundred and twenty princes, which should be over the whole kingdom; And over these three presidents; of whom Daniel was first: that the princes might give accounts unto them, and the king should have no damage." – Daniel 6:1-2

King Darius left Daniel in his previous position that was given to him by Nebuchadnezzar, who had appointed him over all the astrologers, Chaldeans, and soothsayers. When the Persians took over, the Magi would have been under Daniel's command. The reason they knew where to look for the Messiah is because somewhere down the line Daniel told them where they need to look and when they needed to look.

By God's law, Daniel was a righteous man. He did what he was supposed to do, but under man's law, he had a criminal record. If you recall, King Darius issued a decree, which he later regretted, that no one could pray to God or any other god for thirty days. Daniel not only disobeyed the King's decree, but he opened the windows and prayed three times a day just as he had been doing previously. Daniel was found guilty and tossed into the lion's den, where the angel of the Lord shows up and keeps him company through the night. Because of Daniel's obedience, the king issues a new decree and demands that everyone worship the God of Daniel.

Jonah – Here we have another prophet that got himself into trouble, but this time it was with God. God asked Jonah to go preach to his enemies, but Jonah refused to go because he knew they would repent and God would spare them. Just imagine telling God that you're not only not going to do what He wants you to do, but you're not going to do it because you have a vengeful attitude and you know God is forgiving.

Jonah hopped on a ship and headed the opposite direction of where God wanted him to go. Now, not only is he saying no, but he is also taking action in opposition to God's will. Jonah still ended up in Nineveh, preaching to the people, and the people did indeed repent for what they had done. Jonah was completely unwilling to do God's work, but God still used him to save the lives of all the people in Nineveh.

Peter – Peter is probably the most famous disciple in the Bible, but his record isn't squeaky clean either. Remember when Jesus and the disciples were in the garden, as Judas approached with the guards to arrest Jesus? Peter was the one that pulled his sword and cut off a man's ear.

In modern times, Peter would have gotten hard time in prison, for resisting arrest, aiding and abetting a criminal, and assaulting an officer, regardless if Jesus put his ear back on or not.

Later in Acts 12:7 we find Peter breaking out of prison with the help of the Angel of the Lord. Again, in modern time, that would have made him a fugitive.

Mary Magdalene – She was a former prostitute that followed Jesus. Prostitution was a highly unfavorable profession among the Jews because it was common among the worship of pagan gods. It was also a violation of Jewish law. Interestingly though, Mary was one of the first people Jesus revealed Himself too after the resurrection. This is important because in those days the testimony of a woman wasn't considered reliable, but she was the one of the first to bring the good news of the resurrection to the disciples.

Paul – Paul makes his dramatic introduction in the book of Acts, at the stoning of Stephen, the first Christian martyr. I'm almost sure, but not positive that Paul, who was then known as Saul, had something to do with the death of Stephen.

Saul was ruthless when it came to hunting down Christians. He kicked in doors, drug people out of the house, and probably participated in the killings. In fact, when he first converted to Christianity, nobody believed him. Everyone thought it was a trap set up in order to kill more Christians.

Paul had a hand in killing God's people, but God still chose to use Paul, and now he has one of the most recognizable names in Christianity, along with Jesus and Peter.

What Should We Take From This?

- Of all the people God could have chosen to be friends with, He chose a drinker, a thief, a liar, a murderer, a man who committed incest, a sex offender, a stuttering man, a cripple, a fugitive, an adulterer, a covetous man, a man that disobeyed authority, a grudge holder, an unwilling man, someone that disturbed the peace, a man that resisted arrest, and someone that persecuted Christians, as the people He wanted to do His will.

- If God can look past our faults, we need to learn to look past the faults of others as well.

- If God can use the people listed above, and He usually does, He can and will use us, no matter what we have done in the past.

Chapters Of Interest

- Genesis 6
- Genesis 12

Verses To Remember

"Discretion shall preserve thee, understanding shall keep thee: To deliver thee from the way of the evil man, from the man that speaketh froward things; Who leave the paths of uprightness, to walk in the ways of darkness"

Proverbs 2:11-13

"He hath shewed thee, O man, what is good; and what doth the LORD require of thee, but to do justly, and to love mercy, and to walk humbly with thy God?"

Micah 6:8

Chapter 6: Jesus And Religion

This chapter is for those of you who believe being religious will somehow get you to heaven or means you have a better relationship with God than someone who doesn't lead a religious life. Religion should be an outward sign of your inward relationship with Christ. When Jesus walked on this earth, His biggest enemies were religious leaders, known as the Pharisees and Sadducees.

The Pharisees and Sadducees were all Jewish, but they differed in what they believed, just like the body of Christ does today. The Pharisees believed in the resurrection of the dead, and the Sadducees didn't. Those were their two major denominations.

In Christianity today, we have Protestant, Catholic, 7th Day Adventists, Mormonism, Pre-Trib, Mid-Trib, Post-Trib, Non Denomination, COGIC, etc. That's way too many denominations for any sane person to want to keep up with. Christianity has split up and gone in too many different directions over the last 2,000 years, and it has all been because of the church leaders.

The problem comes into play when you start to add books to the Bible, make up your own religious doctrine and practices, take verses out of context, and keep people from reading the true word of God. If every Christian actually read their Bible and stopped believing every person that stands in the pulpit, based simply on a title, there would be a lot fewer mislead Christians. Even the Bereans didn't just believe Paul (Acts 17:11). They referenced everything he said, but sadly, most Christians today don't do that. Jesus Himself warns us of false religious leaders.

> ❖ "But while men slept, his enemy came and sowed tares among the wheat, and went his way." - Matthew 13:25

Jesus wasn't talking about grass; He was talking about the bad being mixed in among the good, and the church specifically. There are religious leaders that don't want people to know the truth, and people out there that think going to church, taking communion, shouting, and saying, "Praise God" every Sunday is how you gain salvation.

> ❖ "Not every one that saith unto me, Lord, Lord, shall enter into the kingdom of heaven; but he that doeth the will of my Father which is in heaven." - Matthew 7:21

The hard but very real truth is, there are some people sitting in church right now, that will probably spend eternity in hell because they are more focused on being religious than having a relationship with Jesus Christ.

The Devil Is In The Details

Sometimes the details are what lead us off the right path to a relationship with God. Most Christians don't consider that their theological or religious position could be wrong; even though that's the way they were raised. Believing something your entire life doesn't make it the right belief. Jesus was trying to get this point across to the Pharisees and Sadducees, all throughout the Gospel.

> ❖ "Ye blind guides, which strain at a gnat, and swallow a camel." - Matthew 23:24

The Pharisees and Sadducees were so caught up in the religious details, that they didn't see the big picture that was right in front of them. They had been looking for the Messiah their entire life and He was standing right in front of their faces, but they couldn't see Him because He was more focused on relationship than religion.

In the Jewish system of worship, sacrifices were how you restored your relationship with God, and had your sins forgiven. Now, instead of sacrifices, certain denominations want you to do things to be forgiven for your sins, such as, giving money, chanting, saying "Hail Mary" a certain number of times, and many other unnecessary practices. The truth is, asking God for forgiveness through Jesus Christ, is the only way to be forgiven.

> ❖ "And Samuel said, Hath the LORD as great delight in burnt offerings and sacrifices, as in obeying the voice of the LORD? Behold, to obey is better than sacrifice, and to hearken than the fat of rams." - 1 Samuel 15:22

> ❖ "Will the LORD be pleased with thousands of rams, or with ten thousands of rivers of oil? shall I give my firstborn for my transgression, the fruit of my body for the sin of my soul? He hath shewed thee, O man, what is good; and what doth the LORD require of thee, but to do justly, and to love mercy, and to walk humbly with thy God?" - Micah 6:7-8

God isn't really all that concerned about every little detail in our Christian walk, because He wants us to focus on the big picture, an actual relationship with Him. In these few verses, God is completely clear on what He wants from us: listen to Him, obey his voice, do the right thing, love mercy, and walk with Him.

> ❖ "I will not reprove thee for thy sacrifices or thy burnt offerings, to have been continually before me. I will take no bullock out of thy house, nor he goats out of thy folds. For every beast of the forest is mine, and the cattle upon a thousand hills. I know all the fowls of the mountains: and the wild beasts of the field are mine. If I were hungry, I would not tell thee: for the world is mine, and the fullness thereof. Will I eat the flesh of bulls, or drink the blood of goats? Offer unto God thanksgiving; and pay thy vows unto the most High: And call upon me in the day of trouble: I will deliver thee, and thou shalt glorify me." - Psalm 50:8-15

God was making the point that it isn't sacrifices that corrects our sin because He doesn't need anything from us. Sacrificing was an act of obedience. At the end of the verse God tells us that He wants us to call on Him when we need Him, praise Him when He delivers us, and give Him the glory.

> ❖ "Draw nigh to God, and he will draw nigh to you. Cleanse your hands, ye sinners; and purify your hearts, ye double minded." - James 4:8

You can listen without obeying, which I don't suggest. I knew at sixteen that I was supposed to be sharing the Word of God with the world, but here I am, twenty-six, and just now doing what God told me to do. As a result, I've lost a lot, been to jail three times, and was on probation for three years. Now that I've started walking back in the right direction, things are changing for the better so I can't do anything but praise God for that. If I had been obedient to begin with I could have avoided a lot of what I went through.

> **Point To Ponder:** The first step in obedience is choosing to listen to God. You have to hear Him before you can obey Him.

The People Pleasers

Another huge problem in the body of Christ is that some of our leaders are trying too hard to please people. We don't teach the book of Revelation because people don't want to hear about the end of the world. We don't talk about specific sins because it might offend someone. We only preach feel good sermons because we don't want people to stop coming to service. As Ministers of God's Word, we are held accountable for everything we do teach, and also everything we choose not to teach. As members of the body of Christ, we are all held accountable for not knowing God's word, when all we have to do is open it up and read it.

The Pharisees and Sadducees were people pleasers, and Jesus wasn't a big fan of it. They wore flashy robes, said extra long prayers in public, and put on a show when they were fasting, so that people would see how "holy" they were.

> ❖ "And when thou prayest, thou shalt not be as the hypocrites are: for they love to pray standing in the synagogues and in the corners of the streets, that they may be seen of men. Verily I say unto you, They have their reward." - Matthew 6:5

> ❖ "Moreover when ye fast, be not, as the hypocrites, of a sad countenance: for they disfigure their faces, that they may appear unto men to fast. Verily I say unto you, They have their reward." - Matthew 6:16

Contrary to popular belief, a hypocrite is not someone that says one thing and does another, but it is someone who says or does one thing and believes another. In New Testament times, the word *hypokrites* was used to refer to stage actors. Jesus was in fact calling the religious leaders of His time, nothing but actors.

> ❖ "He answered and said unto them, Well hath Esaias prophesied of you hypocrites, as it is written, This people honoureth me with their lips, but their heart is far from me." – Mark 7:6

As the verse points out, the religious leaders were putting on a show. On the outside they praised and worshipped God, but on the inside they had no desire to know God. That is what a hypocrite really is.

Religious Extortion

In Jesus' day, religious extortion was big business, and so it has remained for the last 2,000 or so years since He walked on the earth. We see it all the time, and it has given religion, specifically Christianity a bad name. Jesus didn't go around soliciting financial seeds, prayer rugs, blessed envelopes, and all sorts of other magically enchanted items in order to make a profit. In fact, it was quite the opposite because Jesus condemned such actions.

> ❖ "And Jesus went into the temple of God, and cast out all them that sold and bought in the temple, and overthrew the tables of the moneychangers, and the seats of them that sold doves, and said unto them, It is written, My house shall be called the house of prayer; but ye have made it a den of thieves." – Matthew 21:13

The moneychangers were extorting the parishioners in order to make a profit on sacrifices. They were literally selling forgiveness. According to the Old Testament law, the Jews needed to make sacrifices in order to be forgiven. For those that didn't raise animals, they would have to purchase the animals to sacrifice, but the moneychangers were inflating the prices to increase their profits.

God's house has once again become a den of thieves. Although, not every church falls into these practices, please be very cautious about any church that is more focused on getting money out of your pocket than getting God's Word into your spirit. Tithes are important in running a church, because bills do need to be paid, but it shouldn't be the only sermon you hear every Sunday. Tithes don't lead to salvation.

There is also something else very interesting that goes on at a lot of churches that simply doesn't make sense to me. The practice of making the members get up and walk up to the front, so everyone can see who is and isn't paying their tithes. This appears to be more for show than anything else. Jesus also condemned this practice a long time ago.

> ❖ "Take heed that ye do not your alms before men, to be seen of them: otherwise ye have no reward of your Father which is in heaven. Therefore when thou doest thine alms, do not sound a trumpet before thee, as the hypocrites do in the synagogues and in the streets, that they may have glory of men. Verily I say unto you, They have their reward. But when thou doest alms, let not thy left hand know what thy right hand doeth: That thine alms may be in secret: and thy Father which seeth in secret himself shall reward thee openly." - Matthew 6:1-4

Jesus makes it very clear that our offerings are supposed to be a private, not a public matter. In fact, he goes as far as to say that your left hand shouldn't even know what your right hand is doing because it should just be between you and God. Just be mindful of Jesus' teachings when you present your tithes.

Holier Than Thou

I'm sure you've heard the expression, "holier than thou" used to describe some church folk. It refers to the member that always talks about what they don't do, never did, how they always pay their tithes on time, etc. I personally can't relate to being the perfect Christian because I'm not, and it doesn't seem like Jesus had much to say to the Pharisees and Sadducees that felt this way about themselves.

Think back to the last chapter and you'll remember that some of God's closest friends were murderers and thieves, and the one of the two innocent men, Joseph, was convicted and went to prison for a sex crime. Jesus hung out with those that the Scribes, Pharisees, and Sadducees looked down on. In fact, Jesus made it a habit to hang out with beggars, cripples, tax collectors, prostitutes, and even on the cross, one of His last acts was to promise a thief salvation, so why is it that some of the most religious people look down on everyone else?

> ❖ "Woe unto you, scribes and Pharisees, hypocrites! for ye make clean the outside of the cup and of the platter, but within they are full of extortion and excess. Thou blind Pharisee, cleanse first that which is within the cup and platter, that the outside of them may be clean also. Woe unto you, scribes and Pharisees, hypocrites! for ye are like unto whited sepulchres, which indeed appear beautiful outward, but are within full of dead men's bones, and of all uncleanness. Even so ye also outwardly appear righteous unto men, but within ye are full of hypocrisy and iniquity." – Matthew 23:25-28

On the Inside, some of our religious leaders and church members aren't right with God, but on the outside, they have it all together.

> ➤ **Point To Ponder:** If you have everything together without God, what do you need God for?

The truth is God doesn't help those that can help themselves; He helps those that realize they need His help. Jesus sums it up nicely.

> ❖ "And it came to pass, as Jesus sat at meat in the house, behold, many publicans and sinners came and sat down with him and his disciples. And when the Pharisees saw it, they said unto his disciples, Why eateth your Master with publicans and sinners? But when Jesus heard that, he said unto them, they that be whole need not a physician, but they that are sick." – Matthew 9:10-12

Most people don't go to a doctor if they don't have a problem, unless it's a routine check up, which serves the purpose of preventing future problems. As humans, we are all sick with the disease of sin, to which there is only one cure, Jesus Christ. If you believe you've got it all together and you don't sin, there is nothing God wants to use you for. He is looking for those humble enough to admit that they need His help.

> **Point To Ponder:** You can't be humble before God unless you get off your high horse.

Religion vs. Relationship

The Scribes, Pharisees, and Sadducees were focused on their religious appearance because they wanted to be praised by men for being so holy. On the other hand, the people Jesus hung around with were already rejects for the most part, so they really didn't have much to lose, as far as popular opinion was concerned.

The religious leaders wanted Jesus to be like them, to sit in high places, and be honored by men, but Jesus was only concerned with honoring the Father in heaven. Jesus lifted up and encouraged those that were brought low by religious and social standards. Again, Jesus words give us a lot more insight into why Jesus kept the company He did.

> ❖ "But go ye and learn what that meaneth, I will have mercy, and not sacrifice: for I am not come to call the righteous, but sinners to repentance." - Matthew 9:13

God likes to hang out with sinners, but if you don't agree, I challenge you to find the list of perfect people He hung out with. God the Father hung out with sinners in the Old Testament and Jesus hung out with them all the time in the New Testament. Maybe you're still not convinced that God isn't that much into religion, so consider the Temple and the priests. God only let the High Priest come into the Holy of Holies, where the presence of God dwelled, once a year. On the other hand, God ate with Abraham (the pimp), He wrestled with Jacob (the thief), He walked with Adam (the disobedient son), He talked to David (a murdering, covetous, adulterer), and He talked with Moses (a murdering fugitive) face to face as a man talks with his friend (Exodus 33:11).

The religious leaders knew of Jesus, but they didn't know Him personally. They knew His name, where He was from, and what He taught, but they didn't know him personally. The disciples on the other hand knew Jesus personally; they ate with Him, drank with Him, slept with Him, walked with Him, and they talked with Him.

The difference between religion and relationship is exactly what Jesus was pointing out in His ministry. He didn't come to bring peace and harmony the first time, He came to divide the humble from those full of pride, the sheep from the goats, those that love Him from those that don't, and most of all religion from relationship.

> ❖ "Suppose ye that I am come to give peace on earth? I tell you, Nay; but rather division: For from henceforth there shall be five in one house divided, three against two, and two against three. The father shall be divided against the son, and the son against the father; the mother against the daughter, and the daughter against the mother; the mother in law against her daughter in law, and the daughter in law against her mother in law." - Luke 12:51-53

Killing In The Name Of God

I've always found it interesting that some of the most brutal wars start because of religion. People claim to represent God or a god of peace, but they are not peaceful themselves. I'm not talking about Satanists that sacrifice people, but people who profess to know the God of the Bible. God has never had a "convert or die" policy, at least not in Judaism or Christianity. I also find it interesting that I've never heard of anything on the level of the Crusades, started in the name of the Devil.

> ➤ **Point To Ponder:** Satanists have probably killed less people throughout history than Christians.

When the long awaited Messiah finally came to Israel, it was the religious leaders and the Sanhedrin Counsel members that wanted Him dead, not the common folk. Jesus took away the crowds from the Pharisees, Sadducees, and Scribes. He was teaching relationship instead of religion, and that didn't sit well with the religious leaders of that time. Jesus healed on Sunday; He spoke with more authority, so the religious leaders tried to set Him up on several occasions. When all else failed, they demanded that He be put to death, as required by their law, because He claimed to be the Son of God. The common folk didn't get on board with His crucifixion until the Pharisees and Sadducees convinced them. That is a perfect example of blind religion. The people saw Jesus everyday and never had a problem with Him, but in the end they choose religious belief over their relationship with Him.

> ❖ "But the chief priests moved the people, that he should rather release Barabbas unto them. And Pilate answered and said again unto them, What will ye then that I shall do unto him whom ye call the King of the Jews? And they cried out again, Crucify him. Then Pilate said unto them, Why, what evil hath he done? And they cried out the more exceedingly, Crucify him." - Mark 15:11-14

Religion is what blinded the Scribes, Pharisees, and Sadducees, and they eventually blinded the people that followed them. God is not an ordinary God, and He doesn't always operate how you would expect Him to. Sometimes He switches things up, but religious tradition doesn't have room for anything out of the ordinary or outside of the box. Religion is the main thing keeping us separated from God.

Just think for a minute, Lucifer was the ultimate religious leader. Him and the rest of the angels had absolute proof of God and what He could do. They could go to God directly, yet Lucifer somehow managed to convince his congregation of angels to rebel against God. Those of us who are called to lead God's people need to be very careful of how we use our influence over the flock. Those of us who attend church as the congregation need to be attentive to what is being taught because it is easy for a leader to turn into the next David Koresh or Jim Jones if we have not been studying to show ourselves approved.

Chapter 6

What Can We Do To Fix Things?

Reading The Bible - Some people say that if we read the Bible every day, and meditate on God's Word, everything will be all right. Well, that's a start. We should indeed know God's Word, but that alone won't fix our relationship with God or bring us salvation. The Devil knows God's word and meditates on it. When he tempted Eve in the garden, he quoted part of God's message, but twisted it to his advantage (Genesis 3:1). He also quotes Psalm 91:12 to Jesus during the temptation in the wilderness:

> ❖ "And saith unto him, If thou be the Son of God, cast thyself down: for it is written, He shall give his angels charge concerning thee: and in their hands they shall bear thee up, lest at any time thou dash thy foot against a stone." – Matthew 4:6

It's obvious that simply knowing God's Word isn't enough to restore our relationship with God.

Believing In God – Some of us think that by believing in God, we automatically have a relationship with Him. While that may be true, it is definitely not a close relationship. It takes more than simply believing in God, to change your relationship with Him.

> ❖ "Thou believest that there is one God; thou doest well: the devils also believe, and tremble." – James 2:19

If we simply believe, we find ourselves in the same boat as the demons. They believe in God, but they are still opposed to God, so again, it's obvious that simply believing in God is not going to cut it.

Tithes and Seed Sowing – Paying your tithes is important because in a properly set up ministry, it helps to pay the church's obligations and goes toward outreach, but you can't buy a relationship with God, regardless of what the man on T.V. is telling you. Jesus didn't walk around collecting seed money in exchange for blessings and heeling. He did quite the opposite; He blessed and healed people for free, based on their faith.

> ❖ "But Jesus turned him about, and when he saw her, he said, Daughter, be of good comfort; thy faith hath made thee whole. And the woman was made whole from that hour." – Matthew 9:22

> ❖ "And Jesus said unto him, Go thy way; thy faith hath made thee whole. And immediately he received his sight, and followed Jesus in the way." – Mark 10:52

In both examples, it was the people's faith that made them whole, not their seeds or their tithes. Another example we need to keep in mind is that the Pharisees paid their tithes, but God didn't reward them for it because they did it for show.

Nobody can offer you blessings in exchange for cash. Seed sowing and tithing are not magical incantations that invoke the mystical power of God, but they are a duty of believers to help further God's kingdom. God has promised to bless us for paying our tithes (10%), and if we are obedient we will receive those blessings.

> ❖ "Bring ye all the tithes into the storehouse, that there may be meat in mine house, and prove me now herewith, saith the LORD of hosts, if I will not open you the windows of heaven, and pour you out a blessing, that there shall not be room enough to receive it." – Malachi 3:10

God has already promised you more blessings than you can imagine if you are obedient. With that said, tithing still won't fix your relationship with God.

So, how exactly do we change or fix our relationship with God? There are seven steps we are going to discuss in the next chapter.

What Should We Take From This?

- Neither God nor Jesus was too concerned with religious traditions or what people think about the company they keep.

Chapter 6

- Jesus came to call the sinners, not those who are already righteous.

Chapters Of Interest

- Matthew 12
- Matthew 16

Verses To Remember

"I love them that love me; and those that seek me early shall find me.

Proverbs 8:17

"Only fear the LORD, and serve him in truth with all your heart: for consider how great things he hath done for you."

1 Saumuel 12:24

Chapter 7: Restoring Your Relationship

Because our relationship with God has been damaged, we need to make a few repairs. There are seven steps that I believe are essential to starting or restoring our relationship with God.

Step One: Recognition

As you have been reading through this book, you have probably recognized that there may be a problem with your relationship with God, and maybe you continued reading in order to find answers to your questions. Sin is a constant problem, and many of us need to continually revisit Step One. Thankfully, you have recognized that there is something wrong, and you are taking the necessary steps to fix it. According to the Bible:

> ❖ "But we are all as an unclean thing, and all our righteousnesses are as filthy rags; and we all do fade as a leaf; and our iniquities, like the wind, have taken us away." – Isaiah 64:6

That's an extremely discouraging verse to read, if you are someone that prides themselves on being a good or righteous person. If you are one of those people, you need to replace that pride with humility, as we discussed in Chapter One. And again, the Bible tells us:

> ❖ "As it is written, There is none righteous, no, not one:" – Romans 3:10

Now that we have directly identified the problem, which is a constant state of sin, we need to move on to Step Two.

Step Two: Decision

We have identified our problem, but now we need to decide if we want to fix that problem. Going through life without fixing your sin, is like having a brand new car with a busted engine. Sure it looks nice on the outside, but the inside is keeping it from being used to its full potential.

The world offers all kinds of solutions to what we as Christians call sin. One of the more popular ideologies is that right and wrong are only relative, but those same people are offended by the idea of murder. They have those feelings of anger because the concept of right and wrong are programmed into our DNA. Certain members of our society just choose to ignore those feelings, and become people such as Hitler, Stalin, Sadaam Hussein, and Jack the Ripper.

Our conscience is our moral alarm that goes off whenever we have done something that offends our inner selves. Now we've come to a crossroad that could determine the outcome of where you spend eternity.

> ❖ "And if it seem evil unto you to serve the LORD, choose you this day whom ye will serve; whether the gods which your fathers served that were on the other side of the flood, or the gods of the Amorites, in whose land ye dwell: but as for me and my house, we will serve the LORD." - Joshua 24:15

> ➤ **Point To Ponder:** Have you ever done something that only you know about, but you still feel guilty inside?

Step Three: Forgiveness

The next step on your journey is asking for forgiveness. When I speak of forgiveness, I'm talking about the forgiveness only Christ can offer you through His sacrifice on the Cross.

> ❖ "Blessed is he whose transgression is forgiven, whose sin is covered." - Psalm 32:1

As you can see, there is also a blessing in being forgiven. The problem most people run into with forgiveness is being able to forgive those who have wronged them in some way. It's a difficult thing to do, but it is necessary to better your relationship with the Lord.

> ❖ "For if ye forgive men their trespasses, your heavenly Father will also forgive you:" - Matthew 6:14

In order to be forgiven, we first need to forgive. God doesn't want anything holding us back from our relationship with Him.

As He was dying on the cross, Jesus forgave the people that killed Him, and asked God to also forgive them, because they weren't aware of what they were doing.

> ❖ "Then said Jesus, Father, forgive them; for they know not what they do. And they parted his raiment, and cast lots." - Luke 23:34

Sometimes people do wrong things to us without even knowing what they have done. At other times, they know full well, but in either case, we are told to forgive them.

Step Four: Have Faith

Once you ask for forgiveness, you must have faith in a few things:

1. Christ died and rose again for our sins.
2. God does what he says He will do.
3. You are indeed forgiven for your past.

Sometimes faith is the hardest thing to have, especially when you are going through hard times. The simple truth is that God is there, even though we can't physically see Him with our eyes. However, we can feel God spiritually when we make the choice to trust Him.

> ❖ "I have not spoken in secret, in a dark place of the earth: I said not unto the seed of Jacob, Seek ye me in vain: I the LORD speak righteousness, I declare things that are right." - Isaiah 45:19

God has been speaking to all of us since the beginning of creation, and has made His presence known to us. We live in a world that is based on science and the ideology that "seeing is believing", but the Bible says:

> ❖ "Jesus saith unto him, Thomas, because thou hast seen me, thou hast believed: blessed are they that have not seen, and yet have believed." - John 20:29

The Bible makes a big deal about faith, because it is one of the most important aspects to our relationship with the Lord. Lets take a look at what faith is:

- Faith is the substance of things hoped for and the evidence of things not seen. (Hebrews 11:1)

The word faith sums up why we believe in what we believe in. Living a good life isn't what makes us good or righteous people, but faith in Christ's death, burial, and resurrection cleanses us from all sin. Almost our entire relationship with God is centered on faith. The word "faith" is mentioned in 231 verses in the Bible, which is perfectly divisible by seven, the number of completion. To understand faith, let's look at what faith is all about.

- Faith has the power to heal (Matthew 9:22)
- Faith allows you to perform miracles (Acts 6:8)
- Faith has the power to purify (Acts 15:9)
- Faith has the power to sanctify (Acts 26:18)
- Faith reveals God's righteousness (Romans 1:17)
- Faith has the power to justify (Romans 3:28)
- Faith establishes the law (Romans 3:31)
- Faith is counted to us for righteousness (Romans 4:5)
- Faith accesses God's grace (Romans 5:2)
- Faith allows us to prophesy (Romans 12:6)
- Faith guides our walk (2 Corinthians 5:7)
- Faith leads to blessing (Galatians 3:9)
- Faith allows us to receive promises of the Spirit (Galatians 3:14)
- Faith makes us children of God (Galatians 3:26)
- Faith leads to salvation (Ephesians 2:8)
- Faith allows Christ to dwell in our hearts (Ephesians 3:17)
- Faith is our shield (Ephesians 6:16)
- Faith is our breast plate (1 Thessalonians 5:8)
- Faith helps us to overcome (1 John 5:4)

This detailed list on faith can be summed up in a single sentence, yet God felt the need to break it down for us to understand. You won't understand that list unless you understand Hebrews 11:1 and vice versa.

> ❖ "Now faith is the substance of things hoped for, the evidence of things not seen." - Hebrews 11:1

Nothing on the list above can be touched, tasted, seen, felt, or smelled without faith. It takes faith to manifest every one of God's promises above. No matter what we do, and no matter how we live our lives, it all comes down to one single verse:

> ❖ "But without faith it is impossible to please him: for he that cometh to God must believe that he is, and that he is a rewarder of them that diligently seek him." - Hebrews 11:6

Faith is an absolute requirement in order to please God, to be rewarded by God, and to find God. Faith also requires you to rely on God for all of your needs. As people, we have the tendency to want to take matters into our own hands, but sometimes God will put us into situations that we can't deliver ourselves out of no matter how hard we try. That is when we have the opportunity to trust Him.

> ❖ "Be still, and know that I am God: I will be exalted among the heathen, I will be exalted in the earth." - Psalm 46:10

Some times when we get busy trying to fix things, we get ourselves into a deeper mess. Just when we get in so deep that we think we're stuck, God wants us to remember to "be still" and trust Him.

> ❖ "And Moses said unto the people, Fear ye not, stand still, and see the salvation of the LORD, which he will shew to you to day: for the Egyptians whom ye have seen to day, ye shall see them again no more for ever. The LORD shall fight for you, and ye shall hold your peace." - Exodus 14:13-14

Moses and the Israelites were in a situation that they couldn't do anything about. They had made their way out of the bondage of Egypt and Pharaoh wanted them dead, but God had other plans in mind. Moses and the Israelites were not equipped to fight their battle, so they had to completely rely on God, and that He would do exactly what He said He would do. They had to have faith.

Faith vs. Works

Some denominations preach faith and some preach works, but what is the truth according to the Bible? Lets take a look at two verses that at first glance seem in opposition to each other.

> ❖ "For by grace are ye saved through faith; and that not of yourselves: it is the gift of God: Not of works, lest any man should boast." - Ephesians 2:8-9

In his letter to the Ephesians, Paul says we are saved through faith and not of works. On the other hand, James tells us that faith without works is dead. So whom do we believe?

> ❖ "For as the body without the spirit is dead, so faith without works is dead also." - James 2:26

When we take time to examine the scripture in its entirety, we learn that both James and Paul are preaching the same message that Christ did. James even expands on this concept a little bit.

> ❖ "Yea, a man may say, Thou hast faith, and I have works: shew me thy faith without thy works, and I will shew thee my faith by my works." - James 2:18

We are indeed saved by faith, but what good is faith if it is kept secret? Jesus clearly taught this concept to His disciples.

> ❖ "No man, when he hath lighted a candle, putteth it in a secret place, neither under a bushel, but on a candlestick, that they which come in may see the light." - Luke 11:33

Jesus was speaking in parables to His disciples about several things all at once. One of them was faith. Just as you don't light a candle to hide its light, you don't hide your faith by not showing it to the world.

Chapter 7

Our salvation is indeed a gift because Christ freely gave it. All we have to do is accept it, or do we? Built into the key elements of salvation is our very first "work", confessing with our mouth. There is indeed ACTION required on our part. We can't just sit this one out.

> ❖ "That if thou shalt confess with thy mouth the Lord Jesus, and shalt believe in thine heart that God hath raised him from the dead, thou shalt be saved." – Romans 10:9

This is where Paul shows that him and James are indeed on the same page. All throughout the Bible, we see examples of faith and works together, and not just one without the other.

Abraham – He believed what God told him, so he took action by first leaving his home and then by being willing to sacrifice Isaac, all based on God's word. We see Abraham's faith through is works.

Moses – He believed that God would deliver Israel from Egypt so he went to Pharaoh on God's behalf. When God parted the Red Sea, Moses raised his staff. Finally, when God gave him the commandments, Moses walked up the mountain. We see Moses faith through his works.

Rahab – She didn't just have faith that the Israelites would spare her life, but she took action by letting them in her house, hiding them, then tying the ribbon in her window when they invaded. We see Rahab's faith through her works.

Elijah – He knew that God was sending a chariot to pick him up and take him to heaven. He didn't just sit around waiting for it to come, but he walked with Elisha to meet the chariot and go home. Again, we see Elijah's faith by his works.

Jesus – He had faith that He could heel the sick, make the blind see, and the lame walk. He also had faith that His death would save mankind, and that when He got up from the dead, He had faith that He would conquer death.

These are only a few examples, but all of these people walked the walk (works), and didn't just talk the talk. It's easy to say that you have faith when you're not on the spot.

Sometimes we are too worried about what our family and friends might think. We need to learn to completely rely on Him in all things, regardless of what others might think, because that is His will concerning us.

Regardless of what your church teaches, the Bible teaches that we are supposed to be lights and we are supposed to share that light. Christianity is not a spectator religion (I'm pretty sure I heard my mom say that). Jesus Himself tells us not once, but twice, what we need to do as Christians. Once in a parable, then once in plain language just incase we missed it the first time.

> ❖ "Go ye therefore into the highways, and as many as ye shall find, bid to the marriage." – Matthew 22:9

> ❖ "Go ye therefore, and teach all nations, baptizing them in the name of the Father, and of the Son, and of the Holy Ghost:" – Matthew 28:19

Jesus gave us three actions (works) that we need to perform as Christians: Go, teach, and baptize. He didn't say sit, watch, and agree. Faith is to be shown, not hidden.

Step Five: Conversations With God

Prayer is like having God's cell phone number. You can reach Him 24/7, and you never have to wait to get through. As Christians, we should be talking to God more often. Praying is more than just asking God for things. As children, most of us learned what I call "the laziest prayer on earth."

"Now I lay me down to sleep. I pray the Lord my soul to keep. If I should die before I wake, I pray the Lord my soul to take."

> ➢ **Point To Ponder:** "God I'm going to sleep, but take me to heaven if I die." That's what that prayer says in plain English.

In my opinion, this prayer is training children to be lazy with their relationship with God, and those children grow into adults that are lazy in their relationship with God. Don't get me wrong, it is a great thing that parents are even teaching their kids to pray in this day and age, but maybe there should be something more personal added to the prayer in order to prepare us to be adults in Christ.

> ❖ "When I was a child, I spake as a child, I understood as a child, I thought as a child: but when I became a man, I put away childish things." - 1 Corinthians 13:11

Why is it that we as Christians go about our day without talking to God, then we expect God to bless us when we toss up a lazy prayer after we are ready to go to sleep. We give God our last on a daily basis, but we never think anything of it. That's not a conversation with God, that's just keeping in touch.

A conversation requires one person to talk and another person to respond, unless you're like me and enjoy talking to yourself. When we pray, we also need to listen. Sometimes it's good to start praying and sit silently just before we say Amen. I find that praying and meditating on the word of God just before bed allows me to sleep better and hear God in my sleep.

The Bible tells us that God speaks to us when we sleep, because that's when we are able to hear His word.

> ❖ "For God speaketh once, yea twice, yet man perceiveth it not. In a dream, in a vision of the night, when deep sleep falleth upon men, in slumberings upon the bed; Then he openeth the ears of men, and sealeth their instruction, That he may withdraw man from his purpose, and hide pride from man." - Job 33:14-17

While we are awake, we are too concerned with what is going on in our lives to listen to God. Even though we should be listening to God first, God is understanding and is willing to wait until our day settles, before He starts speaking. That goes back to pride, and as you notice at the end of verse 17, God waits in order to hide our pride. Talking and listening are both very important to every true relationship, including our relationship with God.

> ❖ "Pray without ceasing." - 1 Thessalonians 5:17

Staying in constant prayer isn't just a good idea, its an essential part of our walk with God. There is true power in prayer when we are sincere in what we are talking to God about. Here is what the Bible says about prayer:

- When we pray, God will listen (Jeremiah 29:12)
- Prayer helps us resist temptation (Mark 14:38)
- Prayer changes things (James 5:16)

Why Doesn't God Answer My Prayers?

That's a pretty common question, and it's based on the assumption that God doesn't simply say, "no" in some cases. Praying to God doesn't mean God is going to grant your request. God is not a genie in a magic lamp that you can rub and get free wishes. Jesus gave the disciples a very detailed lesson on the dos and don'ts of praying. Let's break it down and see what we are doing wrong.

> ❖ "And when thou prayest, thou shalt not be as the hypocrites are: for they love to pray standing in the synagogues and in the corners of the streets, that they may be seen of men. Verily I say unto you, They have their reward." - Matthew 6:5

The religious leaders of the time loved to be seen by men, so they would stand in the streets praying loudly. They weren't praying from their heart, but as a matter of show. That's why Jesus referred to them as "hypocrites" also known in His time, as "stage actors".

> ❖ "But thou, when thou prayest, enter into thy closet, and when thou hast shut thy door, pray to thy Father which is in secret; and thy Father which seeth in secret shall reward thee openly." - Matthew 6:6

Jesus instructs us to pray to God in private and we will be rewarded openly. When we pray in private, we don't have anyone to impress, and we can be sincere with God, in what we are praying for.

> ❖ "But when ye pray, use not vain repetitions, as the heathen do: for they think that they shall be heard for their much speaking. Be not ye therefore like unto them: for your Father knoweth what things ye have need of, before ye ask him." - Matthew 6:7-8

Jesus also warns us against repeating ourselves over and over again, as if asking more than once in the same prayer will produce a different or faster outcome. This also applies to chanting memorized words out of habit, that aren't sincerely coming from your heart. Chanting ten "Hail Mary's" won't change your situation between you and God.

Let me give you an example you can relate to if you have kids. If your kids are constant calling your name and asking the same question over and over again, chances are, you'll get annoyed before you finally give them an answer, even if it is the answer they want. God may not get angry with us for asking over and over again, but I think Jesus' point is, He hears you the first time and He knows what you need before you ask.

> ❖ "After this manner therefore pray ye: Our Father which art in heaven, Hallowed be thy name. Thy kingdom come, Thy will be done in earth, as it is in heaven. Give us this day our daily bread. And forgive us our debts, as we forgive our debtors. And lead us not into temptation, but deliver us from evil: For thine is the kingdom, and the power, and the glory, forever. Amen." - Matthew 6:9-13

The prayer that Jesus teaches the disciples contains a few key elements that should be present every time we pray.

- Address God by His title.
- Show respect to God when you come to Him in prayer.
- Unselfishly ask Him to do His will.
- Thank Him for this day that you have lived.
- Ask for God's forgiveness.
- Express your willingness to forgive others.
- Ask God to keep you from temptations and evil.

That is the prayer of the humble. There is nothing selfish in that prayer that leads only to your personal gain. Try submitting to God when you pray, and not praying as if you control God.

When you begin to submit yourself to God's will, your circumstances will change. Submission also plays a vital role in the next step to restoring your relationship with God.

Can I Pray For Things That I Want?

Of course you can pray for the things you want. Jesus, Himself gives the disciples permission to ask for anything they want in His name, and He promises to do it (John 14:13). James revealed to us why we don't get the things we want, when we ask for them in His name.

> ❖ "Ye ask, and receive not, because ye ask amiss, that ye may consume it upon your lusts." - James 4:3

When we ask, we are asking out of selfishness, which is the exact opposite of how Jesus taught the disciples how to pray. Again, we approach prayer with the attitude that God is some magical Being that sits around waiting to grant wishes.

> ➤ **Point To Ponder:** If the only time someone spoke to you was to ask you to do them a favor, how soon would that get old?

Sometimes the circumstances of the time can give us insight into why Jesus told the disciples they could ask for anything they wanted, and He would do it. The key element we as Christians are missing today is a relationship with Christ. Sure, we're saved, we go to church, we read the Bible, we shout on Sunday, but so what? The disciples didn't shout, and they didn't get dressed up for church, but they did know Jesus. They walked, talked, ate, drank, slept, laughed, cried, and lived with Jesus. They were His friends, and as such, they could ask their friend for anything, and their Friend would do it for them. As Christians, we should desire to walk with Christ just as the disciples did.

> ❖ "Confess your faults one to another, and pray one for another, that ye may be healed. The effectual

> fervent prayer of a righteous man availeth much." - James 5:16

The fervent prayer of the righteous brings results. Throughout the Bible, there are accounts of people who prayed and got major results from their prayers.

1. Joshua prayed for the sun to stand still and it did (Joshua 10:13).
2. Elijah prayed for it not to rain and it didn't for 3 ½ years (James 5:7).
3. Elisha prayed for his servant's eyes to be opened and they were (2 Kings 6:17).
4. Daniel prayed for twenty-one days before an angel showed up and gave him a major prophetic revelation (Daniel 10:12-13).

The Bible definitely makes it clear that prayer should be a regular part of our relationship with God.

Step Six: Resistance

Resisting temptation is pretty hard for some of us to do, or maybe it's just that way for me. There are so many things to try and so little time in which to try them. We all have our thing that allows the Devil to beat us up over and over again, so let me see if I can hit a nail on the head here somewhere.

1. Drugs
2. Alcohol
3. Sex
4. Theft
5. Gambling
6. Wasteful Spending

All of these things have one thing in common, they all cost money, except for number three, sometimes. Drug addicts sometimes steal to get money to fund their next fix. Alcoholics aren't much different from drug addicts. Same problem, different drug, but usually they aren't stealing to get their fix. Paying for sex is much faster than dating if you choose to pursue that avenue of physical contact with someone. People usually steal for money or to fund a habit or addiction. Gambling can be just as bad as drug addiction. People have lost their homes, cars, and marriages to gambling. Finally, the one most of us have a problem with, wasteful spending. We buy things we don't really need. If you already have five pair of black jeans and you need to buy another pair because you see them in the store, you have a problem.

Saying God is intelligent would be the biggest understatement ever made. In all His wisdom, God revealed to Paul the source behind our biggest problems.

> ❖ "For the love of money is the root of all evil: which while some coveted after, they have erred from the faith, and pierced themselves through with many sorrows." - 1 Timothy 6:10

Contrary to popular belief, money is not the root of all evil, it's the "love of money" that is the root of all evil.

> ➢ **Point To Ponder:** At the other end of our habit is someone that stands to gain financially from our problems and addictions.

Thankfully, the Bible tells us how to resist these harmful temptations that so many of us fall into.

> ❖ "Submit yourselves therefore to God. Resist the devil, and he will flee from you." - James 4:7

Yep, that's easier said than done, so what do we do now? If you're not yet sure how to resist, you might want to re-read the previous step, while paying special attention to Mark 14:38. God has given us all the answers we will ever need, and all of the tools to get the job done, but we don't study to show ourselves approved.

> ❖ "Study to shew thyself approved unto God, a workman that needeth not to be ashamed, rightly dividing the word of truth." - 2 Timothy 2:15

Soldiers In The Army Of God

We are referred to in the Bible as soldiers because we are constantly at war with both outside and inside forces. In order to be an equipped and effective soldier, we must know whom we are at war with.

> ❖ "For we wrestle not against flesh and blood, but against principalities, against powers, against the rulers of the darkness of this world, against spiritual wickedness in high places." - Ephesians 6:12

Our battle takes place with spiritual forces, not earthly forces, and because of this, we need spiritual equipment to fight this battle. Ephesians 6 gives us a list of what we need to have in order to survive this spiritual war.

> ❖ "Wherefore take unto you the whole armour of God, that ye may be able to withstand in the evil day, and having done all, to stand." - Ephesians 6:13

1. Girdle of Truth
2. Breastplate of Righteousness
3. Feet covered with the Gospel of Peace
4. Shield of Faith
5. Helmet of Salvation
6. Sword Of The Spirit (Word of God)
7. Pray Always

These seven pieces of armor are all connected by one thing, but I'm not going to get into that just yet.

Step Seven: Praising God

You've found a way to have faith, you've started praying, you're resisting temptation, and suddenly something bad happens that causes you to ask, "God, what did I do wrong?" You don't have to do anything wrong for bad things to happen. If you don't know that yet, check out Job. He did everything right and still everything went wrong, but God gives us the answer.

> ❖ "Knowing this, that the trying of your faith worketh patience." - James 1:3

I was watching a movie the other day, and I wish I could remember the name, but one of the characters said, "if you can't go back, fight your way farther inside." At that time, I didn't know it would end up in this book, but it applies to our life as a soldier for Christ. For me, turning to retreat is not an option, and I've come to far to abandon my post, so I have to fight my way deeper into the battle.

Here comes an idea that sounds completely ridiculous at first, and seems to make no sense, but I can testify that it works. When bad things happen, we need to praise God. If this is the first time you've heard this, and you're asking, "why would I do that?" you're probably in the majority right now. Its not human nature to be thankful for bad things, and as a soldier of Christ, our main battle is first within us, then with the world.

> ❖ "But I see another law in my members, warring against the law of my mind, and bringing me into captivity to the law of sin which is in my members." - Romans 7:23

> ❖ "For the flesh lusteth against the Spirit, and the Spirit against the flesh: and these are contrary the one to the other: so that ye cannot do the things that ye would." - Galatians 5:7

Paul isn't talking about church members, he's talking about his mind and spirit being at war with his body, and not being able to do the things that he should. Again, if we are willing to read, the Bible tells us everything we need to know about what God expects from us.

Now that we've discovered why it's unnatural for us to thank God for the bad things, lets take a look at why we should thank God for the bad things.

> ❖ "In every thing give thanks: for this is the will of God in Christ Jesus concerning you." - 1 Thessalonians 5:18

The most important point the Bible makes in regards to our praising God is that it is the will of God concerning us. When we praise God for EVERYTHING (yes, I'm yelling with letters), we show complete submission to God's will and faith in what God has planned for us.

> ❖ "But thou art holy, O thou that inhabitest the praises of Israel." - Psalm 22:3

David points out that God inhabits Israel's praises, and as adopted children, through Christ's death and resurrection, He inhabits ours also. The point David was making was, when we praise God we literally show up right on God's doorstep.

> ➢ **Point To Ponder:** If we want God to answer the door, all we have to do is show up on His doorstep by praising Him.

Now that we are beginning to see God's plan for our relationship with Him, lets go ahead and tie these seven steps together, using the Scriptures.

Putting It All Together

If you haven't figured it out yet, there is a single, binding, word that ties together all seven steps, and all the armor of God. That word is FAITH. Time to break down how faith works with everything we've learned.

Girdle Of Truth - According to John 8:32, the truth will make us free, and John 17:17 tells us that God's word is truth. God's word is truth, and truth leads to freedom, so where does faith fit in?

> ❖ "So then faith cometh by hearing, and hearing by the word of God." - Romans 10:17

We need to hear the Word of God, in order to obtain faith. We have faith in the Word of God, because it is the truth.

Breastplate Of Righteousness - Faith is counted as righteousness (Romans 4:5), and in order for our prayers to be effective, we must be righteous when we approach God.

> ❖ "Confess your faults one to another, and pray one for another, that ye may be healed. The effectual

fervent prayer of a righteous man availeth much." - James 5:16

Preparation Of The Gospel Of Peace - We are saved through faith in the Gospel (good news) that Christ died and rose again the third day to save mankind from their sins.

> ❖ "And the scripture, foreseeing that God would justify the heathen through faith, preached before the gospel unto Abraham, saying, In thee shall all nations be blessed." - Galatians 3:8

God Himself preached the Gospel to Abraham, and as we know, Abraham believed God (faith), and it was counted to him as righteousness (Romans 4:3).

Shield Of Faith - I'm sure you know how faith is connected to faith, so I won't overload you with more on faith, since there was an entire section dedicated to it, but if you'd like to study faith in depth, read Romans 3, 4, and Hebrews 11.

Helmet Of Salvation - We know that salvation comes through faith, which comes from hearing the Gospel, which is the word of God.

> ❖ "And that from a child thou hast known the holy scriptures, which are able to make thee wise unto salvation through faith which is in Christ Jesus." - 2 Timothy 3:15

> ❖ "Receiving the end of your faith, even the salvation of your souls." - 1 Peter 1:9

Sword Of The Spirit - This is the word of God, which we now know is the truth. This is the only weapon we can use in the war, the Word of God. Again, hearing the Word of God, leads to faith.

> ❖ "For the word of God is quick, and powerful, and sharper than any twoedged sword, piercing even to the dividing asunder of soul and spirit, and of the joints and marrow, and is a discerner of the thoughts and intents of the heart." - Hebrews 4:12

Pray Always – We know that if we are righteous, our prayers make a difference. We also know that we can only be made righteous through our faith in the Gospel, which came by the word of God. Prayer is both a defensive and an offensive measure if you recall Mark 14:38. We are always at war, that is why we are told to pray without ceasing (1 Thessalonians 5:17).

I love how the Bible just wraps everything into a nice little package once we take the time to really sit and study God's word. The only defense against the lies of this world is the truth.

> ❖ "Sanctify them through thy truth: thy word is truth." – John 17:17

> ➢ **Point To Ponder:** Now that you know the truth, what do you plan to do with it?

What Should We Take From This?

- Restoring our relationship with God is the easy part, but taking the first step to do it, is the hard part.

- God is ready for a relationship with us whenever we decide we are ready for a relationship with Him.

- God won't force us to do His will, and that is why Jesus stands at the door and knocks, instead of kicking it in.

Chapters Of Interest

o Ephesians 6

Verses To Remember

"Seek ye the LORD while he may be found, call ye upon him while he is near: Let the wicked forsake his way, and the unrighteous man his thoughts: and let him return unto the LORD, and he will have mercy upon him; and to our God, for he will abundantly pardon. For my thoughts are not your thoughts, neither are your ways my ways, saith the LORD. For as the heavens are higher than the earth, so are my ways higher than your ways, and my thoughts than your thoughts."

Isaiah 55:6-9

"And Samuel said, Hath the LORD as great delight in burnt offerings and sacrifices, as in obeying the voice of the LORD? Behold, to obey is better than sacrifice, and to hearken than the fat of rams."

1 Samuel 15:22

Chapter 8: The Humanity Of God

When I was in high school, I use to hear people on television say that they needed to find themselves. I always thought that was ridiculous because we are always changing our beliefs, morals, and standards, so how can you find yourself? Maybe we never truly find ourselves until we die and Christ reveals Himself to us as He is.

It took me all of my life to learn this next lesson, and although I'm considered young in eyes of most people, I feel like I should have known this a long time ago. In order to understand ourselves, we need to understand God. Think of God like your best friend. Most of us have a best friend, who knows everything about us, and we know everything about them, and we still love them regardless of their faults, and vice versa.

God operates like that, but we don't return the love. When we screw up, God forgives us and our relationship continues. He doesn't love us any less when we sin, because Christ died for our sins. On the other hand, when something we perceive as bad happens, we blame God, we cuss at God, we stop going to church, we stop talking to God, just like little kids when they are mad at their parents. Maybe understanding ourselves will help us understand God better, and understanding God will help us understand ourselves better.

Once we understand that our very existence is proof of a Creator, it takes our faith and relationship with God to an entirely new level. Everything we are made of wants to be reconciled with God. Our entire human existence is spent trying to become more like God in every way possible. Simply look at the direction science and technology are headed and you will see for yourself.

The Human Body

The Bible says that the first man was created in God's image, but what does that really mean? Humans aren't very fast or very strong compared to the rest of life on earth. Even ants can lift about ten times their own body weight. If we're lucky, we may be able to lift twice our own weight.

The design of our body seems to be very efficient. Cover one of your eyes, and then uncover it. Can you tell the difference in perception? I can't imagine the development of our two eyes as a result of a cosmic accident or the blind force of evolution. Our bodies may have changed slightly after the fall of man, but I don't believe they have changed that much. In several places in the Bible, a description of God is given. He has hands, feet, hair, eyes, a mouth, etc. Maybe it's in a perfected form and capable of far more than we are now, but our design is unique to us. When was the last time you saw an ape build a car, airplane, computer, or skyscraper? You haven't and you probably never will unless someone trains it to do those things.

> ❖ "I will praise thee; for I am fearfully and wonderfully made: marvellous are thy works; and that my soul knoweth right well." - Psalm 139:14

Let's talk about DNA very quickly. Most of us have heard the word, but some of us don't really know what it means. In the simplest terms, DNA is the full-length instructions on how to build another you. The sperm and the egg come together, share information from the father and mother, put it together in order, and you are built from scratch. DNA is a blueprint for building life of all kinds, not just people.

God put the instructions right in front of our face, and with all of our knowledge and technology, we still can't build a human or any other animal for that matter. That says a lot about just how complex and unique we are, and the best explanations science can come up with are apes and accidents.

Creativity

Take a look around and I'm sure you'll see something created by man; something that was created to make life easier or more enjoyable for us all. We have a desire to create because God creates. God created the heaven, the earth, and everything on it, and as His children, that desire to create was passed on to us. It's almost like spiritual genetics.

> ❖ "In the beginning God created the heaven and the earth." - Genesis 1:1

If you pay close attention to science, mankind is steadily trying to become more like God. We experiment with genetics, cloning, lab created stones, and we have even built a super collider in hopes of figuring out exactly how the universe began.

The world is always reaching to attain something higher than what we are now, but that void can't be filled without God. The human spirit testifies to God's existence because mankind is trying to reclaim our previous existence, as it was in Eden.

Genesis 1:1 was not when God first started creating. The text refers to a beginning and beginnings mark periods of time. God is eternal and not bound by time. He is, was, and has always been, from everlasting to everlasting (Psalm 90:2). Before God created the earth, He created the angels and wisdom.

> ❖ "Where wast thou when I laid the foundations of the earth? Declare, if thou hast understanding. Who hath laid the measures thereof, if thou knowest? or who hath stretched the line upon it? Whereupon are the foundations thereof fastened? or who laid the corner stone thereof; When the morning stars sang together, and all the sons of God shouted for joy?" – Job 38:4-7

> ❖ "The LORD possessed me in the beginning of his way, before his works of old. I was set up from everlasting, from the beginning, or ever the earth was. When there were no depths, I was brought forth; when there were no fountains abounding with water. Before the mountains were settled, before the hills was I brought forth: While as yet he had not made the earth, nor the fields, nor the highest part of the dust of the world. When he prepared the heavens, I was there: when he set a compass upon the face of the depth: When he established the clouds above: when he strengthened the fountains of the deep: When he gave to the sea his decree, that the waters should not pass his commandment: when he appointed the foundations of the earth: Then I was by him, as one brought up with him: and I was daily his delight, rejoicing always before him; Rejoicing in the habitable part of his earth; and my delights were with the sons of men" – Proverbs 8:22-31

Desire For Knowledge

God is all knowing, which explains why we always want to know more. We read books, take classes, and surf the Internet, all in the pursuit of more knowledge. We have the Discovery Channel, History Channel, Science Channel, Animal Planet, Learning Channel, and a few more, all dedicated to sharing knowledge around the clock.

Each generation will continue to be smarter than the last because it seems as though we are programmed with the desire to be all knowing like God. We won't ever become all knowing, but the desire is written in our DNA.

As you just read above, God created wisdom before He created anything else. Another interesting thing we find in Proverbs is the following verse:

> ❖ "Then I was by him, as one brought up with him: and I was daily his delight, rejoicing always before him;" - Proverbs 8:30

God delighted daily in wisdom. That is why we as humans have a craving for knowledge that seems like it will never be satisfied. In Genesis 11, we find an example of people who wanted to become like the gods. This is more than a story about a simple tower. Skyscrapers are mostly a modern invention, but these people had a level of technology that was probably far beyond our own.

> ❖ "And the LORD said, Behold, the people is one, and they have all one language; and this they begin to do: and now nothing will be restrained from them, which they have imagined to do." - Genesis 11:6

Their level of technology had to have been very high because God Himself expresses that they had become one, having one language, and that they could accomplish anything they imagined and the human imagination is very wild. God destroyed their civilization and scattered them after that. It wasn't their pursuit of knowledge that caused God to put a stop to them; it was what they were doing with that knowledge after they had attained it.

Think about our day and age. With a simple computer program, we can translate any language we want. We all speak a single language, technology. Now, we are trying to crack the secret to DNA, life, and creation, which should be a sign to all that our time is winding down. When the prophet Daniel spoke of the end, he mentioned that we would have a sudden increase of knowledge.

> ❖ "But thou, O Daniel, shut up the words, and seal the book, even to the time of the end: many shall run to and fro, and knowledge shall be increased." - Daniel 12:4

Knowledge will be our downfall because the more we learn; the less people believe we need God. One fact remains, science cannot explore the supernatural world, so it can't provide answers to what happens after we leave this world and move on to the next.

> ❖ "Because that, when they knew God, they glorified him not as God, neither were thankful; but became vain in their imaginations, and their foolish heart was darkened. Professing themselves to be wise, they became fools, And changed the glory of the uncorruptible God into an image made like to corruptible man, and to birds, and fourfooted beasts, and creeping things." - Romans 1:21-23

It sounds as if the Bible is speaking of evolution. We were made in God's image, but our scientific "knowledge" tells us that we came from cosmic sludge, microorganisms, and apes. Yes, evolution sounds completely ridiculous to me too. Genesis tries to drive home the point that evolution wasn't involved in our process, by saying over and over again that everything produced its own kind. Nothing made it into the Bible by accident. Only God would know that thousands of years in the future the story of creation would be challenged and that He would need to reassure us in advance.

Jealousy

Jealousy is not only a human trait, but the Bible tells us that God is a jealous God. He is jealous of anything being put ahead of Him on our list of priorities and worship. This isn't some big secret that God keeps in the Old Testament; He is open and upfront about it.

> ❖ "Thou shalt not bow down thyself to them, nor serve them: for I the LORD thy God am a jealous God, visiting the iniquity of the fathers upon the children unto the third and fourth generation of them that hate me" - Exodus 20:5

It makes sense that God would be jealous, when you consider that He created everything, and He is the only God. Why should He share His spotlight with gods that man creates?

> ❖ "For mine own sake, even for mine own sake, will I do it: for how should my name be polluted? and I will not give my glory unto another." - Isaiah 48:11

Anger

God gets mad, just like we get mad. He gets mad when we sin because sin separates us from Him. He also gets mad when we put other gods before Him or attribute His creation to some random, unguided, accident.

The anger of a parent is a natural reaction to the disobedience of their children. It is not a hateful anger, but a righteous, loving, anger, coming from their desire for their child to do the right thing. When the children of Israel failed to trust and obey God, He got a little upset with them.

> ❖ "Unto whom I sware in my wrath that they should not enter into my rest." - Psalm 95:11

On the other side of that coin, there is God's anger at mankind for worshipping false gods and denying Him the glory of Supreme Ruler of the universe. This kind of anger stems from God's tendency to become a little jealous when we place things before Him.

> ❖ "Because they have forsaken me, and have burned incense unto other gods, that they might provoke me to anger with all the works of their hands;

therefore my wrath shall be kindled against this place, and shall not be quenched." 2 Kings 22:17

Sarcasm

Have you ever noticed how sarcastic some people are? Personally, I love sarcasm and use it every chance I get. I never understood why until I recently noticed it in the Bible, God is very sarcastic. There are several passages of scripture where God is clearly being sarcastic, and asking rhetorical questions.

> ❖ "And he shall say, Where are their gods, their rock in whom they trusted, which did eat the fat of their sacrifices, and drank the wine of their drink offerings? let them rise up and help you, and be your protection." - Deuteronomy 32:37-38

God is angry with the children of Israel for worshipping other gods, but He is clearly being sarcastic when He refers to these gods ability to eat and drink. He also gets a little sarcastic with Job, when Job starts to question God's intentions. God responds with a series of rhetorical questions that He knows Job can't answer, then sums it up with this sarcastic statement"

> ❖ "Knowest thou it, because thou wast then born? or because the number of thy days is great?" - Job 38:21

Loving

God is a very loving Creator. The Bible is very clear on this issue, and puts into perspective the relationship the Creator wants to have with us.

> ❖ "Only the LORD had a delight in thy fathers to love them, and he chose their seed after them, even you above all people, as it is this day." - Deuteronomy 10:15

Paul tells us that God's love for us was proven through the death of Jesus Christ.

> ❖ "But God commendeth his love toward us, in that, while we were yet sinners, Christ died for us." – Romans 5:8

Sense Of Humor

If you pay attention to some of the stories and to some of the things God says in the Bible, you have to believe God has a sense of humor. When the Philistines steal the Ark of the Covenant from Israel and puts it in the temple with their god, Dagon, God starts playing around with the statue.

> ❖ "When the Philistines took the ark of God, they brought it into the house of Dagon, and set it by Dagon. And when they of Ashdod arose early on the morrow, behold, Dagon was fallen upon his face to the earth before the ark of the LORD. And they took Dagon, and set him in his place again. And when they arose early on the morrow morning, behold, Dagon was fallen upon his face to the ground before the ark of the LORD; and the head of Dagon and both the palms of his hands were cut off upon the threshold; only the stump of Dagon was left to him." – 1 Samuel 5:2-4

God could have done anything to the Philistines, but He chose to tip over the statue on one occasion, and cut the head and arms off on another. It wasn't simply God having fun at the expense of the Philistines, but Him foreshadowing what Isaiah would later reveal to us.

> ❖ "I have sworn by myself, the word is gone out of my mouth in righteousness, and shall not return, That unto me every knee shall bow, every tongue shall swear." – Isaiah 45:23

If you look at some of the things in creation, you will also realize that God likes to play jokes. Take the duck billed platypus for example. It's a mammal that has a bill like a duck, but lays eggs like a reptile or bird, and spends most of its time in water. The only thing funnier than the animal itself is the "theory" of how it evolved. I would encourage you to read about the evolution of the platypus. You will get a pretty good laugh at the "science" behind the theory.

In other places in the Bible, we also find God laughing at the plans that man has. There is a saying, "If you want to make God laugh, tell Him your plans."

> ❖ "Why do the heathen rage, and the people imagine a vain thing? The kings of the earth set themselves, and the rulers take counsel together, against the LORD, and against his anointed, saying, Let us break their bands asunder, and cast away their cords from us. He that sitteth in the heavens shall laugh: the LORD shall have them in derision." - Psalm 2:1-4

> ❖ "The wicked plotteth against the just, and gnasheth upon him with his teeth. The LORD shall laugh at him: for he seeth that his day is coming." - Psalm 37:12-14

It seems as though God finds some amusement in our thinking that evil will overcome good in the end. If you really think about it, it is kind of amusing that people actually think at some point they can get rid of God. Just look at our society and the direction it is heading. People are doing just what Psalm 2 said they would do; trying to get rid of God.

Forgiving

No matter what we have done, God is willing to forgive all of our past transgressions. There is nothing we can do to permanently separate us from God, if we are truly willing to repent, and ask for forgiveness.

> ❖ "For thou, Lord, art good, and ready to forgive; and plenteous in mercy unto all them that call upon thee." - Psalm 86:5

John tells us that in order to gain forgiveness, we need to confess our sins to God. We don't have to sit in any confession booth, chant prayers, or pay money; God's forgiveness is free.

> ❖ "If we confess our sins, he is faithful and just to forgive us our sins, and to cleanse us from all unrighteousness." - 1 John 1:9

Pain

When Jesus walked the earth, He was subject to some of the worst pain imaginable. Before His crucifixion, he was whipped with a cat of nine tails. If you've heard of it, but don't exactly know what it is, watch Passion of The Christ. It is usually a whip with metal prongs on the end, designed to rip the flesh from your body.

After the horrific beating, He was slapped, spit on, and had a crown of thorns forced down on His head. If that wasn't enough, he was crucified. Although nails are driven into your wrists and feet, that's not the most painful part. The pain comes into play when you have to pull up on those nails to breathe. Crucifixion forces your body to slowly drown in its own liquid, and there is no way to stop it.

We've all heard the word "excruciating", but most of us don't know that it comes from the word "crux" which is what we call the cross. There was no word to describe how painful being crucified was, so they invented the word excruciating, which means, "to crucify". Keep that in mind next time you hear someone claim they are in excruciating pain. We serve a God that can relate to pain more than most of us walking this earth.

> ❖ But he was wounded for our transgressions, he was bruised for our iniquities: the chastisement of our peace was upon him; and with his stripes we are healed. - Isaiah 53:5

Sleep

The Bible refers to death as sleep almost all of the time. There is also a saying that "sleep is the cousin of death", but why do we sleep? When we sleep, the body repairs itself, but I think there may be more to sleeping than meets the eye.

When we as Christians are baptized, we symbolically die as Christ did, and when we come out of the water, we are born again, just as Christ was resurrected.

> ❖ "Therefore we are buried with him by baptism into death: that like as Christ was raised up from the dead by the glory of the Father, even so we also should walk in newness of life." - Romans 6:4

Wouldn't it be interesting if sleep were the universal testimony to the resurrection of Christ? I believe it may very well be one of God's ways of proving and testifying to His existence. When we go to sleep, we die (figuratively), and when we wake up, we are resurrected (figuratively). I would encourage you to do some research on sleep and find exactly what science has to say about sleep and why we do it. The results will definitely surprise you.

> ❖ "For the invisible things of him from the creation of the world are clearly seen, being understood by the things that are made, even his eternal power and Godhead; so that they are without excuse:" - Romans 1:20

What Should We Take From This?

- God wants all of mankind to know Him, and come to Him, not just as the Creator of all, but also as a friend of all.

- God can relate to our humanity because Christ came to live among us and experience what its like to be human.

> ❖ "And they shall teach no more every man his neighbour, and every man his brother, saying, Know the LORD: for they shall all know me, from the least of them unto the greatest of them, saith the LORD: for I will forgive their iniquity, and I will remember their sin no more." - Jeremiah 31:34

Chapters Of Interest

- The Entire Bible

Afterword

Relationship, dictionary.com states that a relationship is the condition or fact of being related; a connection by blood or marriage; a particular type of connection existing between people related to or having dealings with each other. My relationship with God is that definition; He is my Father, I have a connection by blood, and we have dealings on a daily basis. Before reading this book I never considered my relationship with God, and after reading it I only hope but to better my relationship.

What do we know of relationships? Well to begin they take more than one person. We know that relationships take work, that sometimes we don't always agree with one another, and at times you have to figure out your own way. The thing that differs in our relationship with God is that He has already told us what it is that we need to do and how to do it. Minister Fortson maps out steps to take that may enrich your relationship with God. I am embracing those steps, while not always easy I know that the outcome will be a great reward.

Since attempting to better my relationship with God, things seem a little better; I say a little because I still have work to do. I don't feel like I am experiencing the hard times alone anymore, because I am able to share my burden with Him. What makes the situation even better is that when sharing it with God He can take anything you throw His way, unlike some of our worldly relationships. However, reflect on your worldly relationships, in remembering that the closer you became and the stronger the love and bond grew, the deeper and more important the relationship was to both parties involved.

Now that you have read the book and have equipped yourself with the necessary tools to construct this beautiful relationship with God and the knowledge to enhance it, be on your way. Don't be afraid to experience something that will take or push you to the next level. Be prepared to be forever changed, to become a better person, to want to learn more about God and the bible. May your journey to a better relationship with God be victorious, enlightening, and informative. Be open to new experiences, be honest with yourself, be encouraged to continue your journey and most importantly be blessed.

Sis. Taneka Dickson
Member of Ignited Praise Fellowship

About The Author

Minister Dante Fortson was born November 15, 1982 in Las Vegas, NV, to Pastor Perryetta Lacy. As a child, growing up in his grandparents' house, Minister Dante Fortson had many experiences that have helped shape his belief in God and the supernatural. As a result of a dream one night and hearing his name being called in the house the next morning, he was saved and baptized at a very young age.

Around 8th grade, Minister Fortson developed an interest in UFOs, aliens, and the occult. One night, a life changing demonic experience, left him with a lasting fear of the dark, and led him to start studying the Bible more intensely for an explanation of the events. It has been a little over a decade since Minister Fortson became a student of Bible prophecy. Now, a self-proclaimed expert in demonology, angelology, and the supernatural, he freely shares his knowledge and experience with anyone seeking advice in spiritual matters.

The road to becoming a minister has not been easy for Minister Fortson. He has been through a lot to get to where he is now. Of all of his life experiences, the one single event that led him back to his calling was going to jail December 19, 2008. After 80 days between County and City Jails, he was released, and shortly thereafter, he started his ministry training. To the glory of God, Minister Dante Fortson was licensed as a minister July 26, 2009. Now that he has stepped into his calling, he believes that he can finally do the work he has been called to do since that day he first heard God's voice in his grandparents' house.

God's work through him is just beginning. We can expect to see many more books from this man of God in the very near future. His goal is simple and familiar. Go ye therefore and teach all nations. Through his writing he plans to do just what Jesus commissioned His disciples to do before His ascension.

Post – Reading Assessment

Re-Testing Your Knowledge Of God

Please complete this short quiz after reading the book.

Do you believe that God is forgiving?

- ❑ Yes
- ❑ No

Do you need to have your life in order before coming to God?

- ❑ Yes
- ❑ No

Does God help those that help themselves?

- ❑ Yes
- ❑ No

Does God prefer to use righteous people instead of sinners?

- ❑ Yes
- ❑ No

Is God still answering prayers?

- ❑ Yes
- ❑ No

Are you required to share your faith with others?

- ❑ Yes
- ❑ No

Does God expect us to be religious and follow church tradition?

- ❑ Yes
- ❑ No

Are religion and having a relationship with God different?

- ❑ Yes
- ❑ No

Religion And Relationship

40 Day Workbook

The Purpose Of This Workbook

Depending on what book you've read, it takes 10 – 30 days to develop a new habit, so I've included a 40 day work book, designed to take you through all seven steps of restoring your relationship, on a daily basis. Each day asks eight questions that go hand in hand with Chapter Seven of the book.

1. What Have You Done Wrong Today?

2. Do You Want Forgiveness For Your Wrong Doings Today?

3. Are You Going To Ask God To Forgive You Today?

4. Do You Believe That God Will Forgive You?

5. What Have You Done To Show Your Faith Today?

6. What Have You Prayed For Today?

7. What Temptations Have You Had To Resist Today?

8. What Can You Praise God For Today?

Once you are done with this workbook, you will be able to look back and assess how your relationship with God has developed, what temptations you've faced, and how your faith in God has grown over the last 40 days.

Throughout the Bible, the number 40 represents a period of trial or testing that one must go through before receiving the ultimate promises made to them by God. In Noah's time it rained for 40 days and 40 nights before coming to an end. The Hebrews wandered through the desert for 40 years before reaching the Promised Land.

Prayerfully, this workbook will force you to be more honest with yourself and God, about your day-to-day actions. My hope is that you will form a new habit of daily recognition and repentance of your sins. As you get use to talking to God on a daily basis, you will begin to notice small changes that will affect your everyday life.

This workbook is not something you can just "get out of the way" early in the morning. You need to wait until the end of your day so you can reflect on everything you have gone through, during the course of your day. If you end your day with your mind on Christ, forgiveness, and a willingness to do better, your renewed relationship with God will begin to come into focus.

If you choose to accept this challenge, you will be forced to take an honest look in the spiritual mirror. You will be force to confront your daily downfalls, and finally, you will be forced to make a decision whether or not you want to restore or begin your relationship with God.

Religion and Relationship - Initial Assessment Test

Section 1 - Yes or No Questions

Please answer the following questions completely and honestly.

Do you pray when you wake up in the morning?

- ☐ Yes
- ☐ No

Do you pray throughout your day?

- ☐ Yes
- ☐ No

Do you pray before you go to sleep at night?

- ☐ Yes
- ☐ No

Do you wait for an answer after you pray?

- ☐ Yes
- ☐ No

Do you believe God will answer your prayers?

- ☐ Yes
- ☐ No

Do you prefer to give in to temptation?

- ☐ Yes
- ☐ No

Do you pray for God to help you through temptation?

- ☐ Yes
- ☐ No

Do you think your daily good deeds out weigh your daily bad deeds?

- ☐ Yes
- ☐ No

Religion and Relationship – Initial Assessment Test

Section 2 – All About The Numbers

Please circle only one answer. Use your best estimation.

How many times per day do you pray?

- ❏ 1-3
- ❏ 4-7
- ❏ 7+

How often do you sin per day?

- ❏ 1-5
- ❏ 6-10
- ❏ 11+

How many times do you ask for forgiveness per day?

- ❏ 1-3
- ❏ 4-7
- ❏ 7+

How many good deeds do you do per day?

- ❏ 1-5
- ❏ 6-10
- ❏ 11+

How many blessings do you actually count per day?

- ❏ 1-5
- ❏ 6-10
- ❏ 11+

Appendix A

Day 1

What Have You Done Wrong Today?   Total Sins Committed ____

_____
_____

Have You Forgiven Those Who Have Wronged You Today?

- ☐ Yes
- ☐ No

Are You Going To Ask God To Forgive You Today?

- ☐ Yes
- ☐ No

Do You Believe That God Will Forgive You?

- ☐ Yes
- ☐ No

How Did You Show Your Faith Today?   Total Good Deeds ____

_____
_____

What Have You Prayed For Today?   Total Times Prayed ____

_____
_____

What Temptations Have You Had To Resist Today?

_____
_____

What Can You Praise God For Today?

_____
_____

Day 2

What Have You Done Wrong Today? Total Sins Committed ____

_____
_____

Have You Forgiven Those Who Have Wronged You Today?

- ❑ Yes
- ❑ No

Are You Going To Ask God To Forgive You Today?

- ❑ Yes
- ❑ No

Do You Believe That God Will Forgive You?

- ❑ Yes
- ❑ No

How Did You Show Your Faith Today? Total Good Deeds ____

_____
_____

What Have You Prayed For Today? Total Times Prayed ____

_____
_____

What Temptations Have You Had To Resist Today?

_____
_____

What Can You Praise God For Today?

_____
_____

Day 3

What Have You Done Wrong Today? Total Sins Committed ____

_____

_____

Have You Forgiven Those Who Have Wronged You Today?

- ❏ Yes
- ❏ No

Are You Going To Ask God To Forgive You Today?

- ❏ Yes
- ❏ No

Do You Believe That God Will Forgive You?

- ❏ Yes
- ❏ No

How Did You Show Your Faith Today? Total Good Deeds ____

_____

_____

What Have You Prayed For Today? Total Times Prayed ____

_____

_____

What Temptations Have You Had To Resist Today?

_____

_____

What Can You Praise God For Today?

_____

_____

Day 4

What Have You Done Wrong Today?   Total Sins Committed ____

_____
_____
_____

Have You Forgiven Those Who Have Wronged You Today?

- ❏ Yes
- ❏ No

Are You Going To Ask God To Forgive You Today?

- ❏ Yes
- ❏ No

Do You Believe That God Will Forgive You?

- ❏ Yes
- ❏ No

How Did You Show Your Faith Today?   Total Good Deeds ____

_____
_____
_____

What Have You Prayed For Today?   Total Times Prayed ____

_____
_____
_____

What Temptations Have You Had To Resist Today?

_____
_____
_____

What Can You Praise God For Today?

_____
_____

Day 5

What Have You Done Wrong Today?   Total Sins Committed ____

_____

_____

Have You Forgiven Those Who Have Wronged You Today?

- ❏ Yes
- ❏ No

Are You Going To Ask God To Forgive You Today?

- ❏ Yes
- ❏ No

Do You Believe That God Will Forgive You?

- ❏ Yes
- ❏ No

How Did You Show Your Faith Today?   Total Good Deeds ____

_____

_____

What Have You Prayed For Today?   Total Times Prayed ____

_____

_____

What Temptations Have You Had To Resist Today?

_____

_____

What Can You Praise God For Today?

_____

_____

Day 6

What Have You Done Wrong Today?   Total Sins Committed _____

_____
_____

Have You Forgiven Those Who Have Wronged You Today?

- ❏ Yes
- ❏ No

Are You Going To Ask God To Forgive You Today?

- ❏ Yes
- ❏ No

Do You Believe That God Will Forgive You?

- ❏ Yes
- ❏ No

How Did You Show Your Faith Today?   Total Good Deeds _____

_____
_____

What Have You Prayed For Today?   Total Times Prayed _____

_____
_____

What Temptations Have You Had To Resist Today?

_____
_____

What Can You Praise God For Today?

_____
_____

Day 7

What Have You Done Wrong Today?   Total Sins Committed ____

_____

_____

Have You Forgiven Those Who Have Wronged You Today?

- ☐ Yes
- ☐ No

Are You Going To Ask God To Forgive You Today?

- ☐ Yes
- ☐ No

Do You Believe That God Will Forgive You?

- ☐ Yes
- ☐ No

How Did You Show Your Faith Today?   Total Good Deeds ____

_____

_____

What Have You Prayed For Today?   Total Times Prayed ____

_____

_____

What Temptations Have You Had To Resist Today?

_____

_____

What Can You Praise God For Today?

_____

_____

Day 8

What Have You Done Wrong Today?   Total Sins Committed ____

_____
_____
_____

Have You Forgiven Those Who Have Wronged You Today?

- ❏ Yes
- ❏ No

Are You Going To Ask God To Forgive You Today?

- ❏ Yes
- ❏ No

Do You Believe That God Will Forgive You?

- ❏ Yes
- ❏ No

How Did You Show Your Faith Today?   Total Good Deeds ____

_____
_____
_____

What Have You Prayed For Today?   Total Times Prayed ____

_____
_____
_____

What Temptations Have You Had To Resist Today?

_____
_____
_____

What Can You Praise God For Today?

_____
_____

Day 9

What Have You Done Wrong Today? Total Sins Committed ____

_____
_____

Have You Forgiven Those Who Have Wronged You Today?

- ☐ Yes
- ☐ No

Are You Going To Ask God To Forgive You Today?

- ☐ Yes
- ☐ No

Do You Believe That God Will Forgive You?

- ☐ Yes
- ☐ No

How Did You Show Your Faith Today? Total Good Deeds ____

_____
_____

What Have You Prayed For Today? Total Times Prayed ____

_____
_____

What Temptations Have You Had To Resist Today?

_____
_____

What Can You Praise God For Today?

_____
_____

Day 10

What Have You Done Wrong Today?   Total Sins Committed ____

_____
_____

Have You Forgiven Those Who Have Wronged You Today?

- ❏ Yes
- ❏ No

Are You Going To Ask God To Forgive You Today?

- ❏ Yes
- ❏ No

Do You Believe That God Will Forgive You?

- ❏ Yes
- ❏ No

How Did You Show Your Faith Today?   Total Good Deeds ____

_____
_____

What Have You Prayed For Today?   Total Times Prayed ____

_____
_____

What Temptations Have You Had To Resist Today?

_____
_____

What Can You Praise God For Today?

_____
_____

Day 11

What Have You Done Wrong Today?   Total Sins Committed ____

_____

_____

Have You Forgiven Those Who Have Wronged You Today?

- ❑ Yes
- ❑ No

Are You Going To Ask God To Forgive You Today?

- ❑ Yes
- ❑ No

Do You Believe That God Will Forgive You?

- ❑ Yes
- ❑ No

How Did You Show Your Faith Today?   Total Good Deeds ____

_____

_____

What Have You Prayed For Today?   Total Times Prayed ____

_____

_____

What Temptations Have You Had To Resist Today?

_____

_____

What Can You Praise God For Today?

_____

_____

Day 12

What Have You Done Wrong Today?   Total Sins Committed ____

_____
_____
_____

Have You Forgiven Those Who Have Wronged You Today?

- ❏ Yes
- ❏ No

Are You Going To Ask God To Forgive You Today?

- ❏ Yes
- ❏ No

Do You Believe That God Will Forgive You?

- ❏ Yes
- ❏ No

How Did You Show Your Faith Today?   Total Good Deeds ____

_____
_____
_____

What Have You Prayed For Today?   Total Times Prayed ____

_____
_____
_____

What Temptations Have You Had To Resist Today?

_____
_____
_____

What Can You Praise God For Today?

_____
_____

Day 13

What Have You Done Wrong Today? Total Sins Committed ____

_____

_____

Have You Forgiven Those Who Have Wronged You Today?

- ☐ Yes
- ☐ No

Are You Going To Ask God To Forgive You Today?

- ☐ Yes
- ☐ No

Do You Believe That God Will Forgive You?

- ☐ Yes
- ☐ No

How Did You Show Your Faith Today? Total Good Deeds ____

_____

_____

What Have You Prayed For Today? Total Times Prayed ____

_____

_____

What Temptations Have You Had To Resist Today?

_____

_____

What Can You Praise God For Today?

_____

_____

Day 14

What Have You Done Wrong Today?   Total Sins Committed ____

_____
_____

Have You Forgiven Those Who Have Wronged You Today?

- ❏ Yes
- ❏ No

Are You Going To Ask God To Forgive You Today?

- ❏ Yes
- ❏ No

Do You Believe That God Will Forgive You?

- ❏ Yes
- ❏ No

How Did You Show Your Faith Today?   Total Good Deeds ____

_____
_____

What Have You Prayed For Today?   Total Times Prayed ____

_____
_____

What Temptations Have You Had To Resist Today?

_____
_____

What Can You Praise God For Today?

_____
_____

Day 15

What Have You Done Wrong Today?   Total Sins Committed ____

_____
_____

Have You Forgiven Those Who Have Wronged You Today?

- ❏ Yes
- ❏ No

Are You Going To Ask God To Forgive You Today?

- ❏ Yes
- ❏ No

Do You Believe That God Will Forgive You?

- ❏ Yes
- ❏ No

How Did You Show Your Faith Today?   Total Good Deeds ____

_____
_____

What Have You Prayed For Today?   Total Times Prayed ____

_____
_____

What Temptations Have You Had To Resist Today?

_____
_____

What Can You Praise God For Today?

_____
_____

Day 16

What Have You Done Wrong Today?　　　Total Sins Committed _____

_____

_____

Have You Forgiven Those Who Have Wronged You Today?

- ❏ Yes
- ❏ No

Are You Going To Ask God To Forgive You Today?

- ❏ Yes
- ❏ No

Do You Believe That God Will Forgive You?

- ❏ Yes
- ❏ No

How Did You Show Your Faith Today?　　　Total Good Deeds _____

_____

_____

What Have You Prayed For Today?　　　Total Times Prayed _____

_____

_____

What Temptations Have You Had To Resist Today?

_____

_____

What Can You Praise God For Today?

_____

_____

Day 17

What Have You Done Wrong Today?   Total Sins Committed ____

_____
_____

Have You Forgiven Those Who Have Wronged You Today?

- ❏ Yes
- ❏ No

Are You Going To Ask God To Forgive You Today?

- ❏ Yes
- ❏ No

Do You Believe That God Will Forgive You?

- ❏ Yes
- ❏ No

How Did You Show Your Faith Today?   Total Good Deeds ____

_____
_____

What Have You Prayed For Today?   Total Times Prayed ____

_____
_____

What Temptations Have You Had To Resist Today?

_____
_____

What Can You Praise God For Today?

_____
_____

Day 18

What Have You Done Wrong Today?   Total Sins Committed _____

_____

_____

Have You Forgiven Those Who Have Wronged You Today?

- ❑ Yes
- ❑ No

Are You Going To Ask God To Forgive You Today?

- ❑ Yes
- ❑ No

Do You Believe That God Will Forgive You?

- ❑ Yes
- ❑ No

How Did You Show Your Faith Today?   Total Good Deeds _____

_____

_____

What Have You Prayed For Today?   Total Times Prayed _____

_____

_____

What Temptations Have You Had To Resist Today?

_____

_____

What Can You Praise God For Today?

_____

_____

Day 19

What Have You Done Wrong Today?   Total Sins Committed ____

_____
_____

Have You Forgiven Those Who Have Wronged You Today?

- ☐ Yes
- ☐ No

Are You Going To Ask God To Forgive You Today?

- ☐ Yes
- ☐ No

Do You Believe That God Will Forgive You?

- ☐ Yes
- ☐ No

How Did You Show Your Faith Today?   Total Good Deeds ____

_____
_____

What Have You Prayed For Today?   Total Times Prayed ____

_____
_____

What Temptations Have You Had To Resist Today?

_____
_____

What Can You Praise God For Today?

_____
_____

Day 20

What Have You Done Wrong Today?   Total Sins Committed ____

_____
_____

Have You Forgiven Those Who Have Wronged You Today?

- ❏ Yes
- ❏ No

Are You Going To Ask God To Forgive You Today?

- ❏ Yes
- ❏ No

Do You Believe That God Will Forgive You?

- ❏ Yes
- ❏ No

How Did You Show Your Faith Today?   Total Good Deeds ____

_____
_____

What Have You Prayed For Today?   Total Times Prayed ____

_____
_____

What Temptations Have You Had To Resist Today?

_____
_____

What Can You Praise God For Today?

_____
_____

Day 21

What Have You Done Wrong Today?   Total Sins Committed ____

_____
_____

Have You Forgiven Those Who Have Wronged You Today?

- ❏ Yes
- ❏ No

Are You Going To Ask God To Forgive You Today?

- ❏ Yes
- ❏ No

Do You Believe That God Will Forgive You?

- ❏ Yes
- ❏ No

How Did You Show Your Faith Today?   Total Good Deeds ____

_____
_____

What Have You Prayed For Today?   Total Times Prayed ____

_____
_____

What Temptations Have You Had To Resist Today?

_____
_____

What Can You Praise God For Today?

_____
_____

Day 22

What Have You Done Wrong Today?   Total Sins Committed ____

_____

_____

Have You Forgiven Those Who Have Wronged You Today?

- ❏ Yes
- ❏ No

Are You Going To Ask God To Forgive You Today?

- ❏ Yes
- ❏ No

Do You Believe That God Will Forgive You?

- ❏ Yes
- ❏ No

How Did You Show Your Faith Today?   Total Good Deeds ____

_____

_____

What Have You Prayed For Today?   Total Times Prayed ____

_____

_____

What Temptations Have You Had To Resist Today?

_____

_____

What Can You Praise God For Today?

_____

_____

Day 23

What Have You Done Wrong Today?   Total Sins Committed _____

_____

_____

Have You Forgiven Those Who Have Wronged You Today?

- ❏ Yes
- ❏ No

Are You Going To Ask God To Forgive You Today?

- ❏ Yes
- ❏ No

Do You Believe That God Will Forgive You?

- ❏ Yes
- ❏ No

How Did You Show Your Faith Today?   Total Good Deeds _____

_____

_____

What Have You Prayed For Today?   Total Times Prayed _____

_____

_____

What Temptations Have You Had To Resist Today?

_____

_____

What Can You Praise God For Today?

_____

_____

Day 24

What Have You Done Wrong Today?   Total Sins Committed _____

_____

_____

Have You Forgiven Those Who Have Wronged You Today?

- ❏ Yes
- ❏ No

Are You Going To Ask God To Forgive You Today?

- ❏ Yes
- ❏ No

Do You Believe That God Will Forgive You?

- ❏ Yes
- ❏ No

How Did You Show Your Faith Today?   Total Good Deeds _____

_____

_____

What Have You Prayed For Today?   Total Times Prayed _____

_____

_____

What Temptations Have You Had To Resist Today?

_____

_____

What Can You Praise God For Today?

_____

_____

Day 25

What Have You Done Wrong Today?   Total Sins Committed ____

_____

_____

Have You Forgiven Those Who Have Wronged You Today?

- ☐ Yes
- ☐ No

Are You Going To Ask God To Forgive You Today?

- ☐ Yes
- ☐ No

Do You Believe That God Will Forgive You?

- ☐ Yes
- ☐ No

How Did You Show Your Faith Today?   Total Good Deeds ____

_____

_____

What Have You Prayed For Today?   Total Times Prayed ____

_____

_____

What Temptations Have You Had To Resist Today?

_____

_____

What Can You Praise God For Today?

_____

_____

Day 26

What Have You Done Wrong Today?   Total Sins Committed ____

_____
_____

Have You Forgiven Those Who Have Wronged You Today?

- ❏ Yes
- ❏ No

Are You Going To Ask God To Forgive You Today?

- ❏ Yes
- ❏ No

Do You Believe That God Will Forgive You?

- ❏ Yes
- ❏ No

How Did You Show Your Faith Today?   Total Good Deeds ____

_____
_____

What Have You Prayed For Today?   Total Times Prayed ____

_____
_____

What Temptations Have You Had To Resist Today?

_____
_____

What Can You Praise God For Today?

_____
_____

Day 27

What Have You Done Wrong Today?   Total Sins Committed ____

_____

_____

Have You Forgiven Those Who Have Wronged You Today?

- ❏ Yes
- ❏ No

Are You Going To Ask God To Forgive You Today?

- ❏ Yes
- ❏ No

Do You Believe That God Will Forgive You?

- ❏ Yes
- ❏ No

How Did You Show Your Faith Today?   Total Good Deeds ____

_____

_____

What Have You Prayed For Today?   Total Times Prayed ____

_____

_____

What Temptations Have You Had To Resist Today?

_____

_____

What Can You Praise God For Today?

_____

_____

Day 28

What Have You Done Wrong Today?   Total Sins Committed _____

_____
_____

Have You Forgiven Those Who Have Wronged You Today?

- ❑ Yes
- ❑ No

Are You Going To Ask God To Forgive You Today?

- ❑ Yes
- ❑ No

Do You Believe That God Will Forgive You?

- ❑ Yes
- ❑ No

How Did You Show Your Faith Today?   Total Good Deeds _____

_____
_____

What Have You Prayed For Today?   Total Times Prayed _____

_____
_____

What Temptations Have You Had To Resist Today?

_____
_____

What Can You Praise God For Today?

_____
_____

Day 29

What Have You Done Wrong Today?   Total Sins Committed _____

_____

_____

Have You Forgiven Those Who Have Wronged You Today?

- ❑ Yes
- ❑ No

Are You Going To Ask God To Forgive You Today?

- ❑ Yes
- ❑ No

Do You Believe That God Will Forgive You?

- ❑ Yes
- ❑ No

How Did You Show Your Faith Today?   Total Good Deeds _____

_____

_____

What Have You Prayed For Today?   Total Times Prayed _____

_____

_____

What Temptations Have You Had To Resist Today?

_____

_____

What Can You Praise God For Today?

_____

_____

Day 30

What Have You Done Wrong Today?   Total Sins Committed _____

_____

_____

Have You Forgiven Those Who Have Wronged You Today?

- ❏ Yes
- ❏ No

Are You Going To Ask God To Forgive You Today?

- ❏ Yes
- ❏ No

Do You Believe That God Will Forgive You?

- ❏ Yes
- ❏ No

How Did You Show Your Faith Today?   Total Good Deeds _____

_____

_____

What Have You Prayed For Today?   Total Times Prayed _____

_____

_____

What Temptations Have You Had To Resist Today?

_____

_____

What Can You Praise God For Today?

_____

_____

Day 31

What Have You Done Wrong Today?   Total Sins Committed ____

_____

_____

Have You Forgiven Those Who Have Wronged You Today?

- ❑ Yes
- ❑ No

Are You Going To Ask God To Forgive You Today?

- ❑ Yes
- ❑ No

Do You Believe That God Will Forgive You?

- ❑ Yes
- ❑ No

How Did You Show Your Faith Today?   Total Good Deeds ____

_____

_____

What Have You Prayed For Today?   Total Times Prayed ____

_____

_____

What Temptations Have You Had To Resist Today?

_____

_____

What Can You Praise God For Today?

_____

_____

Day 32

What Have You Done Wrong Today?   Total Sins Committed ____

_____

_____

Have You Forgiven Those Who Have Wronged You Today?

- ❑ Yes
- ❑ No

Are You Going To Ask God To Forgive You Today?

- ❑ Yes
- ❑ No

Do You Believe That God Will Forgive You?

- ❑ Yes
- ❑ No

How Did You Show Your Faith Today?   Total Good Deeds ____

_____

_____

What Have You Prayed For Today?   Total Times Prayed ____

_____

_____

_____

What Temptations Have You Had To Resist Today?

_____

_____

What Can You Praise God For Today?

_____

_____

Day 33

What Have You Done Wrong Today?   Total Sins Committed ____

_____
_____

Have You Forgiven Those Who Have Wronged You Today?

- ❏ Yes
- ❏ No

Are You Going To Ask God To Forgive You Today?

- ❏ Yes
- ❏ No

Do You Believe That God Will Forgive You?

- ❏ Yes
- ❏ No

How Did You Show Your Faith Today?   Total Good Deeds ____

_____
_____

What Have You Prayed For Today?   Total Times Prayed ____

_____
_____

What Temptations Have You Had To Resist Today?

_____
_____

What Can You Praise God For Today?

_____
_____

Day 34

What Have You Done Wrong Today?   Total Sins Committed ____

_____
_____

Have You Forgiven Those Who Have Wronged You Today?

- ❏ Yes
- ❏ No

Are You Going To Ask God To Forgive You Today?

- ❏ Yes
- ❏ No

Do You Believe That God Will Forgive You?

- ❏ Yes
- ❏ No

How Did You Show Your Faith Today?   Total Good Deeds ____

_____
_____

What Have You Prayed For Today?   Total Times Prayed ____

_____
_____

What Temptations Have You Had To Resist Today?

_____
_____

What Can You Praise God For Today?

_____
_____

Day 35

What Have You Done Wrong Today? Total Sins Committed ____

_____
_____

Have You Forgiven Those Who Have Wronged You Today?

- ☐ Yes
- ☐ No

Are You Going To Ask God To Forgive You Today?

- ☐ Yes
- ☐ No

Do You Believe That God Will Forgive You?

- ☐ Yes
- ☐ No

How Did You Show Your Faith Today? Total Good Deeds ____

_____
_____

What Have You Prayed For Today? Total Times Prayed ____

_____
_____

What Temptations Have You Had To Resist Today?

_____
_____

What Can You Praise God For Today?

_____
_____

Day 36

What Have You Done Wrong Today?   Total Sins Committed _____

_____
_____

Have You Forgiven Those Who Have Wronged You Today?

- ❏ Yes
- ❏ No

Are You Going To Ask God To Forgive You Today?

- ❏ Yes
- ❏ No

Do You Believe That God Will Forgive You?

- ❏ Yes
- ❏ No

How Did You Show Your Faith Today?   Total Good Deeds _____

_____
_____

What Have You Prayed For Today?   Total Times Prayed _____

_____
_____

What Temptations Have You Had To Resist Today?

_____
_____

What Can You Praise God For Today?

_____
_____

Day 37

What Have You Done Wrong Today?   Total Sins Committed ____

_____
_____

Have You Forgiven Those Who Have Wronged You Today?

- ❑ Yes
- ❑ No

Are You Going To Ask God To Forgive You Today?

- ❑ Yes
- ❑ No

Do You Believe That God Will Forgive You?

- ❑ Yes
- ❑ No

How Did You Show Your Faith Today?   Total Good Deeds ____

_____
_____

What Have You Prayed For Today?   Total Times Prayed ____

_____
_____

What Temptations Have You Had To Resist Today?

_____
_____

What Can You Praise God For Today?

_____
_____

Day 38

What Have You Done Wrong Today?　　　Total Sins Committed _____

_____

_____

Have You Forgiven Those Who Have Wronged You Today?

- ❏ Yes
- ❏ No

Are You Going To Ask God To Forgive You Today?

- ❏ Yes
- ❏ No

Do You Believe That God Will Forgive You?

- ❏ Yes
- ❏ No

How Did You Show Your Faith Today?　　　Total Good Deeds _____

_____

_____

What Have You Prayed For Today?　　　Total Times Prayed _____

_____

_____

What Temptations Have You Had To Resist Today?

_____

_____

What Can You Praise God For Today?

_____

_____

Day 39

What Have You Done Wrong Today?   Total Sins Committed ____

_____
_____

Have You Forgiven Those Who Have Wronged You Today?

- ☐ Yes
- ☐ No

Are You Going To Ask God To Forgive You Today?

- ☐ Yes
- ☐ No

Do You Believe That God Will Forgive You?

- ☐ Yes
- ☐ No

How Did You Show Your Faith Today?   Total Good Deeds ____

_____
_____

What Have You Prayed For Today?   Total Times Prayed ____

_____
_____

What Temptations Have You Had To Resist Today?

_____
_____

What Can You Praise God For Today?

_____
_____

Day 40

What Have You Done Wrong Today?   Total Sins Committed ____

_____
_____

Have You Forgiven Those Who Have Wronged You Today?

- ❏ Yes
- ❏ No

Are You Going To Ask God To Forgive You Today?

- ❏ Yes
- ❏ No

Do You Believe That God Will Forgive You?

- ❏ Yes
- ❏ No

How Did You Show Your Faith Today?   Total Good Deeds ____

_____
_____

What Have You Prayed For Today?   Total Times Prayed ____

_____
_____

What Temptations Have You Had To Resist Today?

_____
_____

What Can You Praise God For Today?

_____
_____

Religion and Relationship - Post Assessment Test

Section 1 - Yes or No Questions

Please answer the following questions completely and honestly.

Do you pray when you wake up in the morning?

- Yes
- No

Do you pray throughout your day?

- Yes
- No

Do you pray before you go to sleep at night?

- Yes
- No

Do you wait for an answer after you pray?

- Yes
- No

Do you believe God will answer your prayers?

- Yes
- No

Do you prefer to give in to temptation?

- Yes
- No

Do you pray for God to help you through temptation?

- Yes
- No

Do you think your daily good deeds out weigh your daily bad deeds?

- Yes
- No

Appendix C

Religion and Relationship - Post Assessment Test

Section 2 - All About The Numbers

Please circle only one answer. Use your best estimation.

How many times per day do you pray?

- ☐ 1-3
- ☐ 4-7
- ☐ 7+

How often do you sin per day?

- ☐ 1-5
- ☐ 6-10
- ☐ 11+

How many times do you ask for forgiveness per day?

- ☐ 1-3
- ☐ 4-7
- ☐ 7+

How many good deeds do you do per day?

- ☐ 1-5
- ☐ 6-10
- ☐ 11+

How many blessings do you actually count per day?

- ☐ 1-5
- ☐ 6-10
- ☐ 11+

Now that you've completed your 40 day journey, try comparing your new answers with your old answers and see if you've experienced any spiritual growth. Some of us may be surprised that we've grown, while others may have stayed the same. Keep in mind, that just because this 40 day lesson is over, does not mean that you cannot continue the process on your own. Thank you for taking this journey with me, and I pray that you continue to grow in Christ.

Appendix C

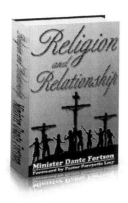

Shop Online And Save Big

Order The Paper Back Version Online And Receive 10% Off!!!

Promotion Code:
G3BSWHVK
www.createspace.com/3397122

Feel free to share your discount with your friends and family.

Get Your Personally Autographed Copy
Only $24.95
www.MinisterFortson.com

Books Make Great Gifts
Buy Copies For Your Family, Friends, and Co-Workers
Only $9.95 + Shipping When You Buy 10 or More
www.MinisterFortson.com

Subscribe To My Monthly Newsletter For FREE!!!
http://feeds.feedburner.com/MinisterFortson

Please Request Religion and Relationship At Your Local Bookstores and Libraries

More From Minister Dante Fortson

Please visit my website and subscribe with your email address to stay updated with my latest news and articles.

You can also drop in and voice your opinion about everything you have just read or any of the other articles on the site. I do my best to provide truthful answers to the tough questions, we as Christians have everyday.

Articles You Might Want To Read

Why Do Bad Things Happen To Good People?
Homosexuality and The Bible
Marijuana and The Bible
The Truth About Shacking up
The Truth About Using Curse Words
NIV vs. KJV: Which Version Is Better?
Adultery According To The Bible

Minister Dante Fortson On The Web

Follow Me On Twitter
twitter.com/ministerfortson

Request Me On MySpace
myspace.com/ministerfortson

Watch Me On You Tube
youtube.com/ministerfortson

The Fall: Rise Of Lucifer

Follow the book from beginning to end. Join myself and Bro. Stanford Greenlee as the writing process unfolds in this three part, epic, Christian Fiction novel. Experience the ups and downs with us as we go from idea to publishing.

Myspace.com/thefallbook

www.MinisterFortson.com

Coming Soon: The Epic Trilogy

Coming Soon: The Prophecy Guide

Prophecy 101
A Prophetic Journey Through The Bible

Minister Dante Fortson

Made in the USA
Lexington, KY
31 October 2013